Dueling Identities

Dueling Identities

The Christian Biker

Doreen Anderson-Facile

LEXINGTON BOOKS

A division of
ROWMAN & LITTLEFIELD PUBLISHERS, INC.
Lanham • Boulder • New York • Toronto • Plymouth, UK

LEXINGTON BOOKS

A division of Rowman & Littlefield Publishers, Inc.
A wholly owned subsidiary of The Rowman & Littlefield Publishing Group, Inc.
4501 Forbes Boulevard, Suite 200
Lanham, MD 20706

Estover Road
Plymouth PL6 7PY
United Kingdom

British Library Cataloguing in Publication Information Available

Library of Congress Cataloging-in-Publication Data

Anderson-Facile, Doreen, 1959–
  Dueling identities : the Christian biker / Doreen Anderson-Facile.
    p. cm.
  Includes bibliographical references.
  ISBN-13: 978-0-7391-1587-9 (cloth : alk. paper)
  ISBN-10: 0-7391-1587-1 (cloth : alk. paper)
  1. Motorcyclists—Religious life. I. Title.
  BV4596.M67A53 2007
  248.8'8—dc22   2007019756

Printed in the United States of America

♾™ The paper used in this publication meets the minimum requirements of American
National Standard for Information Sciences—Permanence of Paper for Printed Library
Materials, ANSI/NISO Z39.48–1992.

This book is dedicated to Jim and Jake.

Contents

Acknowledgements

I would like to thank and acknowledge all the Black Sheep that have supported me through the completion of this book. I am especially grateful to Deb Doran for the ceaseless patience, time, and energy she joyfully provided me in terms of her stenography skills and her unfailing friendship.

With special thanks to:

Janet Kay Anderson, Edna Bonacich, Peter Burke, Robert Nash Parker, Rhonda Dugan, Jami Brown and Jennifer Scroggins.

CHAPTER ONE

The Biker Culture

The Harley-Davidson motorcycle, since its introduction in 1903, has commanded a form of reverence and respect from not only those who ride but also those who admire motorcycles.[1] The popular image of Harley riders is that they are free and unconstrained.[2] A Harley conjures up a lifestyle of untamed, uncivilized freedom similar to that of the "outlaw" cowboy; where men are men and women are the women who love to love them. This image is quite common within the biker world of Harley riders.[3] Many motorcycle enthusiasts believe that the Harley-Davidson is the most excellent motorcycle produced; hence, owning a Harley-Davidson becomes a symbol, represents an image and status in the world of bikers.[4] Owning a Harley-Davidson automatically places the rider into a subculture of riders that has its own specific identity.[5]

The image of an "outlaw" cowboy on a Harley-Davidson motorcycle rather than a horse radiates independence, toughness, and wild freedom that has been perpetuated by the media, entertainment industry, and law enforcement.[6] In the 1960s, Harley riders were portrayed as reckless deviants; they were "rebels without a cause."[7] The early sixties illuminated the Harley rider as a rather sleazy, reckless deviant rider that rebelled against authority and mainstream culture.[8] However, in the late 1980s, the Harley-Davidson Corporation, through creative marketing techniques, minimized the image of bikers as deviant, and the company developed a new image of Harley riders that includes mainstream middle-class individuals who enjoy the freedom of riding a Harley.[9] This transformation has been startling; it is now common to see college professors, doctors, and lawyers decked out in black leather and riding Harleys.[10] This shift in the image of the Harley rider has increased the interest in owning and riding a Harley throughout mainstream America.[11]

Historically, the Harley-Davidson has been a motorcycle deemed high in character, quality, reliability, and power. However, in the late 1960s Harley-Davidson Corporation "ended its sixty two years of private/family management"

1

and was bought out by the American Metal Foundries (AMF).[12] Throughout the next eleven years, while the production system of the AMF/Harley-Davidson modernized and sales increased, the style and the uniqueness of the Harley-Davidson motorcycle quickly declined.[13] "Although some customers remained loyal; AMF/Harley-Davidson lost a lot of money, because the finished motorcycles revealed an increasing number of defects."[14] Due to these changes in ownership and production, the Harley-Davidson motorcycle became ordinary and no longer did the media concern itself with stories of the rough and rugged Harley rider.[15]

In 1981, twelve of the top executives, loyal to the original Harley-Davidson corporation signed a contract to purchase the floundering, if not, unredeemable company from AMF/Harley-Davidson.[16] The next ten years turned out to be the worst years the company had yet encountered. In fact, the corporation asked the International Trade Commission to increase tariffs on the import of foreign bikes to help build the American market; this was accomplished and five years later the tariff was lifted and gave "free reign to competition."[17] In addition, AMF/Harley-Davidson Corporation implemented a variety of marketing and manufacturing principles attempting to save the company including producing metal racks in which to carry Air Force bombs.[18] Probably the most innovative marketing and manufacturing program utilized by Harley-Davidson was the MAN (materials as needed) system. The MAN system reduced over-stock and eliminated storage; manufacturing motorcycles in relation to market demand. This principle not only reduced operation costs, but also limited the surplus on the market, thus allowing for demand to rise.

The manufacturing changes along with creative marketing allowed the Harley-Davidson motorcycle to rise to its previous status. The desire to own a Harley-Davidson and to become part of this subculture increased.[19] Since 1990, Harley-Davidson Corporation has more than quintupled its production of motorcycles from 62,458 motorcycles in 1990 to 329,017 in 2005.[20] The demand for a Harley is so high that the Harley-Davidson Corporation has recently built two new production plants, and has had nineteen consecutive years of record revenues and earnings.[21] In addition to the national market that accounted for 266,507 Harley-Davidson motorcycles shipped in 2005, the global market attracted 62,510 Harley-Davidson motorcycles drawing a fair share of the new Harley's production.[22] Additionally, the desire for a Harley in other parts of the world is also growing.

Along with this increase in sales of Harley-Davidson is a change in the type of person who is purchasing the motorcycle.[23] At one time it was believed that the only people who rode Harleys were "outlaw" bikers who were part of a gang.[24] Now the "outlaw" bikers and "their" women represent only a small portion of the many men and women who ride Harleys.[25] One of the most obvious reasons for this is that the price of a new 2006 Harley ranges from $7,400 for a Sportster (a smaller engine also referred to as a Sporty), to $23,000 and higher for a Touring Bike, an Ultra Classic Electric Glide (the largest Harley made, also referred to as a Hog).[26] In short, a different type of buyer is now prominent on the Harley-Davidson's showroom floors, i.e., the professional, middle- to upper-middle class man or woman (in 2005 those purchasing a Harley were eighty-nine percent males and eleven percent females—up from two percent in 1986), who want to buy into the lifestyle that can be experienced through the ownership of a Harley-Davidson.[27]

In general, the contemporary Harley rider comes from a middle-to-upper-middle-class background. The median income of the people purchasing a Harley-Davidson motorcycle in 2005 was over $80,000 up from $47,300 in 1990.[28] Also, the median age of the Harley buyers has risen from 37 years old in 1990 to 47 years old in 2005.[29] Purchasing a Harley-Davidson motorcycle seemingly creates for the buyer a lifestyle, in particular a cultural identity, and entrance into a subculture of riders that comes merely from ownership of a Harley-Davidson motorcycle.[30] This new group of riders takes on the same type of clothing as that of the "outlaw" biker which they purchase new from Harley Dealerships, through catalogues, from vendors at swap meets and at biker events.[31] Although they attempt to assume the same roles, tough attitudes and rugged appearance of the "outlaw" biker, these new riders are limited, to some extent, by the newness of their clothing and inexperience in the "outlaw" culture. Nevertheless, they seemingly desire to have the same effect on the non-Harley riders: the citizens.[32] What is most interesting is the desire by most "new" Harley riders to be seen as tough and "cool," and they do this through Harley ownership and purchasing Harley accessories. The Harley-Davidson symbol is a cultural icon that represents not only the tough and rough biker but also reflects a middle-to-upper-middle-class lifestyle. In fact, Harley-Davidson parts, accessories, and general merchandise reached just over 1 billion dollars in sales in 2004 ($1,005,333,000).[33] The Harley-Davidson Accessories are purchased by many people regardless of bike ownership.

In 2005, twenty-eight percent of the people purchasing a new Harley-Davidson motorcycle were first time motorcycle buyers or had not owned a motorcycle for at least five years. The willingness to purchase an expensive motorcycle with no riding experience emphasizes the active pursuit of an identity and the desire to make a status statement.[34] The Harley-Davidson is a larger motorcycle, one usually driven by more experienced riders; however buying into the image seems to encourage new riders to jump on to not only a larger bike, but also a more expensive bike. This suggests that riding a Harley-Davidson and being part of this biker group is more about image and identity than actual riding.

There are many different organized groups riding Harley-Davidsons including the Harley Owners Group (HOG), outlaw bikers such as the "Hells Angels," "Mongols," or the "Vagos." Interestingly, there are Christian biker groups, the focus of this book. There are many different Christian motorcycle groups (ministries) including Riders for Christ, Tribe of Judah, Servants for Christ, Soldiers for Jesus, and Set Free. These ministries include all types of bikes (e.g., Honda, BMW, Harley-Davidson, Suzuki, Kawasaki, and Triumph). One Christian motorcycle ministry is Black Sheep Harley-Davidsons for Christ. This motorcycle ministry is unique in regard to other Christian motorcycle ministries because its members own and ride exclusively Harley-Davidson motorcycles. This is specifically highlighted in the Black Sheep Harley-Davidson for Christ's (Black Sheep HDFC) mission statement which states "The ministry of Black Sheep HDFC exists to introduce Jesus Christ to the world of motorcycle riders, for the purpose of making more and better disciples through the ministry of the local church."[35] Black Sheep HDFC began to organize in late 1999 as a single chapter in the Temecula Valley in Southern California with as few as five members and now has approximately twenty-six chapters in seventeen states, over five hundred members and is rapidly growing.[36] The Black Sheep HDFC ministry's principle focus is Harley-Davidson riders, specifically members of the Harley Owners Group (HOG).[37] Harley Owners Group (HOG) is an organization made up of approximately 650,000 Harley-Davidson riders that share a passion for riding Harley-Davidson motorcycles. Membership in the HOG offers group rides, product discounts at authorized Harley-Davidson dealerships, group events and the chance to be part of the "Harley family." The individual HOG chapters are organized through the local dealerships but run by the members.

Black Sheep HDFC is known throughout the "Harley family" as a ministry that provides service at events such as the "Love Ride," Laughlin Run, Primm, Nevada Run, Heart Ride, and other motorcycle events. These events (detailed in chapter four) are usually all day events or weekend events for motorcycle riders, specifically for Harley riders, and consist of group rides, food, parties, music and prizes. Also at these events are booths that sell a variety of items including t-shirts, leather garments, motorcycle parts and other paraphernalia that is of interest to the Harley rider. Black Sheep HDFC members are often serving food at various events, providing worship service at events, offering free motorcycle towing and visiting HOG members in the hospital. They also provide other types of ministry work such as assisting people with yard work, small handyman projects, money and, of course, friendship. The Black Sheep provide chaplaincy services for funerals, weddings, and counseling. They supply food to the local food pantries, and give clothing and blankets to the poor. This motorcycle ministry has monthly meetings, biker church, rallies and group rides throughout California and other areas of the country, with the mission to assist those in need. In short, the Black Sheep HDFC ministry is a motorcycle ministry that seeks to "[introduce] Jesus Christ to the world of motorcycle riders" through service to the biker community.[38]

However, while the motivations of the Black Sheep differ from other Harley riders their outward appearance is the same. The rough leather-clad, tattooed, pony-tailed male members of the Black Sheep look the same as members of hard-core clubs such as the "Hells Angels" or the "Vagos." The distinction between riders has generally not been obvious to most outsiders, who have historically tended to categorize all bikers into one disreputable group. Furthermore, many onlookers have also stereotyped all women involved with Harleys in a negative light, assuming that all biker women are disorderly, promiscuous, uneducated, and poor. The research on bikers, thus far, has supported these stereotypes.[39] These stereotypes are surprising because of the high cost of the Harley-Davidson motorcycle and accessories. The more disreputable "outlaw" gangs were once the groups that were associated with the Harley-Davidson. However, times have changed and the new rider is much more affluent, older, and does not neatly fit those particular stereotypes.[40]

Literature Review

At present there has been very little research on the biker subculture. Most of the research available focused on the "outlaw biker." There is little information or research available on the contemporary biker. This lack of research is most likely due to two reasons. First, "outlaw" bikers have not been interested in being studied and second, the contemporary biker is a rather new phenomenon. The literature review for my work will not only encompass the research on "outlaw" bikers, but it will also include a historical trajectory of the changes in the biker subculture over time. Most of the changes in the biker subculture in the last two decades are a result of the marketing strategies of the Harley-Davidson Corporation.[41] The advertising techniques used since the late 1980s have been focused on the contemporary biker. It was in the late 1980s that Harley-Davidson Corporation capitalized on the romanticized image of the Harley-Davidson motorcycle rider. No longer was the primary purchaser of a Harley an "outlaw" biker or a "saloon" society biker, but rather a middle aged professional.[42] The middle aged professional was being sold, not only, the American made Harley-Davidson motorcycle, but also, the image of the rough and tough biker found through the ownership of the Harley.

The "Outlaw" Biker

Little information is available about "outlaw" biker clubs because of the exclusiveness of the clubs. Outlaw bikers only trust other outlaw bikers. In the literature that is available, the researchers who have focused on "outlaw" bikers indicate that their research was, at times, a "risky undertaking."[43] An "outlaw" club member does not want to be asked questions about any part of his life or the club's affairs; they are not interested in filling out questionnaires or being interviewed. Collecting data on the "outlaw" biker community is difficult at best and seemingly only available to researchers that are willing to actively participate in the community. Most of the researchers in this area have been involved with the biker subculture as participant observers and were able to amass their data via personal experience and through casual interviews with members of the "outlaw" biker community.[44]

As a member of a club, a biker is expected to demonstrate a certain behavior, group consciousness and loyalty to his fellow club members. The club and its members (his brothers) are the most important part of any member's life and at all times they must show their loyalty and respect to both. Respect is confirmed through "right behavior" that consists of "sharing booze, spare parts, money, and some types of women," to live a "righteous" life, which includes, "owning, building, and riding bikes, male superiority, nationalism, white superiority, traditional orientation, and various expressions of individual freedom."[45] Some research has defined this type of lifestyle as "communal."[46] Members consider themselves to be "free people in a world of the un-free," and they are highly dedicated to preserving their lifestyle.[47] "Outlaw" bikers are proud to be part of their club and they wear their "colors" (the club emblem or insignia that is sewn on the back of their "cutaway," a jean jacket with the sleeves cut off) with honor.[48]

"Outlaw" bikers realize that they, like all "outlaw" biker clubs, are outcasts from society, and they respect and value the distinction. They perceive themselves as "social pariahs"[49] and eagerly go out of their way to behave in ways that offend and frighten "conventional citizens." Such behaviors might include public sexual activity or nudity, public urination and defecation, obscene gestures, and various acts of violence or threats of violence.[50] They feel that being part of the outlaw world sets them apart from conventional society and they are fiercely loyal to their way of life.

After loyalty to both his brothers and the club as a whole, an "outlaw" biker holds a strong adoration, perhaps metaphorically speaking, even a religious devotion or worship, to his Harley-Davidson motorcycle. An "outlaw" biker would not consider riding any type of bike other than an American-made Harley-Davidson, which holds a special place of honor within an "outlaw" biker's life (a position greater than that of any woman in his life). To damage or criticize a biker's motorcycle can result in some form of violence. "Deadly fights have resulted from such things as spilling beer on a motorcycle or a jesting remark about one. Many "outlaws" affix a sticker to their motorcycles which says: "If you value your life as much as I value my bike, don't fuck with it."[51]

Saloon Society Biker

Wedged between the "outlaw" motorcycle gangs and the contemporary Harley riders is the rider who looks like a hard-core "outlaw" biker, but is not. These riders wear dirty jeans and black leather, have long hair and beards and overall look like "outlaw" bikers but do not belong to any "outlaw" motorcycle gang. A biker is a person who loves to ride and loves the Harley-Davidson motorcycle. However, until the last two decades most bikers were neither "outlaws" nor professionals, but were part of what is referred to as the "saloon society."[52] The "saloon society" consists of the "outlaw" motorcycle gangs and bikers who frequent the same bars, go to the same parties, and move within the same community—the biker community. Although most "saloon society" bikers do not belong to an "outlaw" motorcycle club and are most likely not part of the professional world, they are in the position to move easily between both worlds. In short, "saloon society" bikers are at home and comfortable in the "saloon society," but they are also participants of mainstream America. It is these bikers, the non-club riders, who traditionally have been the mainstay Harley rider.

Contemporary Biker

Research on the contemporary biker is limited at this time mostly due to its fairly recent induction to the motorcycle world. In light of this, the distinctions between riders are generally not obvious to most outsiders. This more recent addition to the Harley subculture is what I refer to as the contemporary biker. This type of biker is fairly new to the subculture and is often not cognizant of the nuances of the social norms, values, attitudes and behaviors of the biker subculture. Often the contemporary biker relies on media and the movie industry for understanding the ways of the group. This is in large part due to the marketing strategies of the Harley-Davidson Corporation. In fact, the image of the new/contemporary biker is solidly created and perpetuated by the Harley-Davidson Corporation.

The Creation, Preservation, and Perpetuation of an Image

To compensate for the negative image of Harley riders that originated in the 1940s and continued through the 1970s, Harley-Davidson corporation re-invented the image of the Harley rider from "wild bikers and one-percent clubs" to a more romanticized image portrayed in the movie Easy Rider.[53] The transformation of the Harley rider began in the early 1990s with the inception of the "biker event." The biker event are gatherings, usually sponsored by Harley-Davidson in some capacity, featuring bike contests, bike racing, bike exhibits, and a "supermarket of Harley accessories, gadgets and clothes."[54] Although, the Sturgis Motorcycle Rally and Races (originally named the Black Hills Motor Classic) began in 1937 with just a few riders, this event now boasts approximately 300,000 riders a year and has become more popular in conjunction with the other biker events. Other popular bike events that cater to Harley riders include "The River Run" in Laughlin, Nevada, "Biketoberfest" at Daytona Beach, Florida, "Bike Week" at Daytona Beach, Florida, as well as others.[55]

It is at these "bike events" that the new contemporary biker emerged. Many people attend these "bike events" to take part in the racing and other bike competitions, while others attend just to watch the events and be part of the "cultural paradise" of Harley riders. Harley-Davidson Corporation began investing in these "bike events," such as Laughlin River Run, Bike Week in Daytona, Love Ride in California and others, in the 1990s to help establish a more positive image of the Harley rider.[56] While the events are still an atmosphere of wild behavior and wild events the biker image has improved. As a result the media attention at "bike events" has increased and the romanticized image of the contemporary biker is now firmly established.

Harley enthusiasts not only buy the Harley-Davidson motorcycle, but they also buy all the products that go along with the Harley-Davidson biker subculture including leather jackets, chaps, patches, shirts, pants, boots, scarves, and other clothing apparel. A Harley enthusiast can also buy a variety of gadgets with the Harley-Davidson logo including clocks, miniature cars, ashtrays, coffee mugs, pictures, pens, coffee, cigarettes, motor oil, and there are even Harley-Davidson's cafes. In addition, other corporations have also taken advantage of the biker image portrayed through the ownership of a Harley-Davidson motor-cycle including Ford Motor Company. Today, you can buy a Harley-Davidson edition Ford pickup.   A person does not have to be an owner of a Harley-Davidson motorcycle to purchase these items; they just need the desire and the money.

The original biker or Harley-Davidson rider has changed over the past sixty years. Most of the changes in the purchasers and riders of Harley-Davidson mo-torcycles is due to the marketing strategies of the Harley-Davidson Corpora-tion.[57] However, much of the attitudes, dress, norms, and values have remained primarily the same to a certain extent. While the contemporary biker does not live communally or consider their bikes to be more important to them than their loved ones, there is still an overarching attitude of the rogue biker in the con-temporary biker of today because the attitude and the rough and tough biker identity is all part of being part of the Harley-Davidson culture. Individuals and groups looking to be part of the Harley-Davidson Motorcycle culture are look-ing for an identity.[58] This identity is found through the ownership of the Harley-Davidson and many of its products. Interestingly, the Harley-Davidson Motor-cycle culture is merely a group of individuals that want to be part of a culture that can be obtained through the ownership of a Harley-Davidson motorcycle and Harley-Davidson products. "A carefully maintained cult" is how Saladini and Szymezak (1997), artfully describe the ingenious consumer manipulation of the Harley-Davidson Corporation.

Black Sheep HDFC: The Christian Biker

The purpose of this research is to expand the limited body of literature available on the Harley-Davidson motorcycle subculture, examining the new phenomena of Christian motorcycle ministries, in particular, the Black Sheep HDFC. What is unique about this study is that it examines an interesting and rather recent addition to the biker subculture, Christian bikers. Most interesting to this re-search is the paradox, perhaps even the oxymoron, in the term "Christian biker," and what the Christian biker phenomenon actually means within the biker sub-culture and the Christian community. Also of interest is how the Christian biker is both created by the biker community as well as creates and changes the biker community. This research questions the contradictions facing the Christian biker in regard to having the "bad boy" image while simultaneously maintaining the "Christian" image. While seeking to unravel these contradictions of identity facing the Christian biker, this research examines how the "bad boy" styles and attitudes break from the cultural norms commonly found within the Christian community.

This research is framed in identity theory. Identity theory is grounded in Symbolic Interactionism in which the focus is on the processes of interaction both psychologically and sociologically.[59] This theoretical framework examines the mechanisms individuals and groups utilize to develop and maintain their identities. Identity theory recognizes that individuals possess a variety of identities including father, mother, worker, wife, husband, daughter, son, pilot, biker, and so on. Furthermore, the theory explores and elucidates how these particular identities emerge, converge and diverge over time and across situations. Exploratory in nature, this research seeks to shine a spotlight onto a subculture that has thus far been unresearched: the Christian biker. The sociological question of interest is the development and perpetuation of identity. This research examines how the members of Black Sheep HDFC develop the identity of a biker and how this identity is maintained, manipulated, and perpetuated over time.

Notes

1. Hopper and Moore 1983, 1990; Watson 1982; Lyng and Bracey Jr. 1995; Quinn 1987.
2. Quinn 1987; Lyng and Bracey Jr.1995; Jackson and Wilson 1993, Watson 1982, Campbell 1884, 1990.
3. Quinn 1987; Watson 1982; Campbell 1984, 1990; Hopper and Moore 1983, 1990; Jackson and Wilson 1993; Lyng and Bracey Jr.1995; Saladini and Szymezak 1997.
4. Quinn 1987; Jackson and Wilson 1993; Hopper and Moore 1983, 1990; Campbell 1983, 1990; Lyng and Bracey Jr.1995; Klemenic 1993; Saladini and Szymezak 1997.
5. Quinn 1987; Watson 1982; Klemenic 1993, Campbell 1984, 1990; Hopper and Moore 1983, 1990; Jackson and Wilson 1993; Lyng and Bracey Jr.1995; Saladini and Szymezak 1997.
6. Hopper and Moore 1983; Jackson and Wilson 1993; Lyng and Bracey Jr.1995; Quinn 1987; Saladini and Szymezak 1997; Watson 1982.
7. Hopper and Moore 1983; Jackson and Wilson 1993; Lyng and Bracey 1995; Quinn 1987; Saladini and Szymezak 1997; Watson 1982.
8. Hopper and Moore 1983; Jackson and Wilson 1993; Lyng and Bracey Jr.1995; Quinn 1987; Saladini and Szymezak 1997; Watson 1982.
9. Lyng and Bracey Jr.1995; Saladini and Szymezak 1997.
10. Saladini and Szymezak 1997; Klemenic 1993; Lyng and Bracey Jr. 1995.
11. Saladini and Szymezak 1997; Klemenic 1993; Lyng and Bracey Jr. 1995.
12. Saladini and Szymezak; pg 114.
13. Saladini and Szymezak; 1997.
14. Saladini and Szymezak; pg 116.
15. Saladini and Szymezak, 1997; Harley-Davidson 2.
16. Saladini and Szymezak; 1997.
17. Saladini and Szymezak; pg.122.
18. Saladini and Szymezak; 1997.
19. Campbell 1990; Saladini and Szymezak 1997; Klemenic 1993; Lyng and Bracey Jr. 1995.
20. Harley-Davidson Corporate Headquarters financial report 2005, Harley-Davidson 1.
21. Harley-Davidson 1.
22. Harley-Davidson 1.
23. Klememic 1993; Harley-Davidson 3; Lyng and Bracey Jr. 1995.
24. Hopper and Moore 1983, 1990; Campbell 1984, 1990; Quinn 1987; Jackson and Wilson 1993; Saladini and Szymezak 1997.

25. Saladini and Szymezak 1997; (Harley-Davidson 3).

26. Harley-Davidson 4.

27. Harley-Davidson 3.

28. Harley-Davidson 3.

29. Harley-Davidson 3.

30. Campbell 1990; Saladini and Szymezak 1997; Klemenic 1993; Jackson and Wilson 1993; Lyng and Bracey Jr. 1995.

31. Klemenic 1993; Jackson and Wilson 1993; Saladini and Szymezak 1997.

32. Campbell 1990; Saladini and Szymezak 1997; Klemenic 1993; Jackson and Wilson 1993; Lyng and Bracey Jr. 1995.

33. Harley-Davidson 5.

34. Harley-Davidson 3.

35. Edwards, 2003.

36. (Free Methodist Church) Edwards, 2003; Black Sheep HDFC.

37. Edwards, 2003; Black Sheep HDFC.

38. Edwards, 2003.

39. Watson; 1982, Quinn; 1987, Lyng and Bracey; 1995, Hopper and Moore; 1990, 1983, Campbell 1984.

40. Saladini and Szymezak, 1997; Harley-Davidson 3.

41. Saladini and Szymezak, 1997; Harley-Davidson 2.

42. Saladini and Szymezak, 1997; Harley-Davidson 2.

43. Hopper and Moore, 1990; Watson, 1982.

44. Hopper and Moore, 1983, 1990; Quinn, 1987; Watson, 1982.

45. Hopper and Moore, 1990; Watson, 1982.

46. Hopper and More, 1983, 1990; Quinn 1987.

47. Watson, 1982.

48. Lyng and Bracey, 1995; Quinn, 1987.

49. Quinn, 1987.

50. Watson 1982.

51. Hopper and Moore, 1990.

52. Quinn, 1987.

53. Saladini and Szymezak; pg 206.

54. Saladini and Szymezak; pg 206.

55. Saladini and Szymezak; pg 189.

56. Saladini and Szymezak, 1997; Harley-Davidson 2.

57. Saladini and Szymezak, 1997; Harley-Davidson 2.

58. Saladini and Szymezak, 1997; Jackson and Wilson, 1993; Lyng and Bracey Jr. 1995; Quinn, 1987.

59. Blumer 1969; Outhwaite and Bottomore, (1994).

CHAPTER TWO

Theoretical Perspective

The theoretical framework for my work lies in structural symbolic interactionist perspective, specifically identity theory. Identity theory traces its historical roots beginning primarily with the work of George Herbert Mead and Herbert Blumer and their theories of symbolic interactionism, followed by the work on self and identity established by Peter J. Burke, Jan Stets, Sheldon Stryker, and Richard Serpe. While the macro-level theories within sociology focus on institutions and their overarching influences on the social world, the micro-level theories within symbolic interactionism focus on the individual (self), personal interaction and how the repetition of behavior affects the social institutions (i.e. law and polity, economy, family, education, religion, government). Identity theory centers on the degree of commitment individuals bring to a role identity and this degree of commitment is theoretically tied to the choices individuals make in any given situation. This chapter outlines identity theory and then applies the theory to how individuals (Christian bikers specifically) function in everyday life forming and restructuring the various roles in which they identify as part of who they are as individuals. Specific to this work will be the examination of how Christian bikers develop a hierarchy of role identities in which both the identity of biker and Christian have a high degree of commitment. This degree of commitment will be seen through Black Sheep membership, biker activities and events, Christian activities and events and the overlap between them.

Theories of Symbolic Interactionism

Symbolic interactionism concentrates on the common set of symbols and know-ledge that provide a framework, a way of knowing, for people within a group or society.[1] Symbols, simply put, are anything in which groups and individuals assign meanings including objects, gestures, people, colors, sounds, languages or any and everything else.[2] Symbols are the agreed upon ways in which individuals and groups communicate and transmit culture, values, norms, and beliefs within a group or society.[3] Over time and across social context, symbols are transmitted through verbal and non-verbal forms of communication and thus create meaning for groups and the larger society.

Paramount to understanding the theories within symbolic interactionism is the principle of the "definition of the situation." In 1928, W.I. Thomas stated his famous Thomas Theorem: "If men define situations as real, they are real in their consequences."[4] If individuals believe something to be true or real, then their actions will support this truth or reality. This can be seen more clearly if one considers how a child will react to being told they are a "bad" or a poor student; if the judgment is stated often enough and the student constructs support for the judgment, whether valid or not, he or she will come to believe in its validity and will respond accordingly.[5] While often the definition of the situation is used to understand deviance (i.e. labeling theory or self-fulfilling prophecy) and forms of discrimination, it can also be used to understand how all people define their everyday life experiences. Randall Collins suggests that the definition of the situation "does not merely apply to these instances of discrimination and failure of achievement. It indicates a principle of how the entire social structure is put together, both in its positive and dominant aspects as well as in its negative and subordinate ones."[6]

Also important in symbolic interactionism is looking at self concept through role performance and Mead's generalized other. The "generalized other" is a concept developed by Mead (1938) and is defined as the ability of individuals and groups to view themselves through the lenses of those who watch them. In other words, it is the ability of an individual to see herself or himself as others do. As a result, the development of the self is defined and refined as individuals define themselves through the eyes of others.[7] By using the "generalized other" as a mirror to interpret one's performance in any given situation, an individual can manipulate their presentation to the world around them to portray themselves in a manner that fits their identity standard. If individuals and groups interpret meaning from the social world around them then they must utilize the social world and the individuals and groups within the social world as a mirror to reflect back on themselves,[8] or as Mead puts it "the generalized other."[9]

Herbert Blumer's Symbolic Interactionism

Blumer's work centers on how individuals create reality in everyday life. He stresses the role of the mind in defining and redefining social situations. He maintains it is how individuals interpret the social situation in which they are engaged that determines their reaction to it. Individuals interpret social situations by evaluating not only themselves within the situation, but also by imagining how others evaluate them. In short, Blumer's theory maintains that all action is mapped out and considered through the interpretation or definition of the situation. To expand upon W. I. Thomas and later George Herbert Mead, Blumer defines the "definition of a situation" by utilizing three basic fundamental premises.

The first premise states that "Human beings act toward things on the basis of the meanings which these things have for them."[10] This means that objects, whether material or non-material, are given meaning via the action taken toward them, and suggests that things of the world must be defined before they have any human meaning or reality. In fact, Randall Collins states "Everything that people act upon or that has an impact upon them must go through the process of subjective meaning."[11] Therefore, meaning of things, whether material or non-material, are constantly being defined, redefined or confirmed.

Blumer's second premise focuses on how meaning given to objects is not only subjective and individual, but also a reflection of the social world. Blumer's second premise is, "The meaning of a thing for a person grows out of the ways in which other persons act toward the person with regard to the thing."[12] Within this second premise one can see the obvious ties to George Herbert Mead and his theory of the "generalized other." This implies that meaning is derived from both the social and psychological world. If meaning is driven both psychologically and sociologically, then the meanings must, to a certain point, be at least ever changing because meanings are in a constant state of definition and redefinition.

Blumer's third premise maintains that all meanings for individuals and groups "occur through a process of interpretation."[13] This interpretation must constantly readjust to the social situation or "the definition of the situation." It is through this interpretation that individuals and groups accept, reject, or readjust their understanding, or "definition of the situation" in any given social situation. If the social situation does not support the individual or groups' meaning or "definition of the situation" then it is either rejected or manipulated in a way that provides agreed upon social meaning.

Individuals and groups must jointly utilize these premises to interpret each situation and determine appropriate action or response. Society exists only in response to human action and agency.[14] The components that make up a society such as roles, social institutions, and values do not exist without the influence of human behavior.[15] Society is not an objective or autonomous force, it is a representation of the people that live and interact within its boundaries.[16] Therefore, as individuals and groups live and interact in society they are simultaneously influencing and interpreting the "social situation" or society.

Important to understanding Blumer's work is to recognize that he views individuals as constantly reevaluating or redefining situations. While some events or situations may be reoccurring and therefore common, individuals will still utilize these three premises. Blumer concludes, therefore, that reinterpretation is always possible if not probable, meaning that any and every situation has the potential for reinterpretation regardless of its commonness.

Identity Theory

Stets and Burke[17] rework the theoretical concept of the "definition of the situation" and include how identity and role choice are developed and maintained through interaction. Consistent with Blumer's work, Stets and Burke[18] contend that individuals are constantly reacting and remolding their self image as it pertains to their interpretation of the "definition of the situation" in which they are engaged. For the purpose of my work, identity theory provides the framework used to further understand the behaviors and motivations of the members of the Black Sheep Harley-Davidsons for Christ Motorcycle Ministry. This theoretical framework offers insight into how an individual develops and maintains the identities of Christian, biker, Christian biker, and Black Sheep member by specifically utilizing the theoretical concepts of identity, commitment, identity salience, and self knowledge.

Identity theory contends that all individuals have multiple identities that make up the "self," these identities are either ascribed, achieved or chosen.[19] Stets and Burke maintain that the self is part of a processual entity in which individuals are able to view themselves through their interactions with others and modify their behavior to better perform the role or, if necessary, reject the role.[20] It is within these interactions that individuals manipulate their self-image; interestingly this manipulation of the self image is done both internally and externally. "Humans have the ability to reflect back upon themselves, taking themselves as objects."[21] Therefore, actors (individuals) are able to view themselves objectively and adjust both their internal view of themselves and the external view that others see. In fact, similar to Cooley's looking glass self,[22] social psychologists from the structural approach contend that individuals are able to "take account of themselves and plan accordingly to bring about future states, to be self aware or achieve consciousness with respect to their own existence."[23]

However, contemporary self theory adds to these concepts by asserting that there is a "multiplicity of selves or a differentiated self composed of multiple aspects rather than a unitary self."[24] The self is, in fact, a set of selves that are "tied to positions and imbued with shared expectations for social action."[25] For example, an individual may have the status of mother, wife, sister, daughter, employee, president of the church guild, member of the animal humane society, teacher, and customer. The status position of sister and daughter are ascribed; the other statuses are most likely either achieved or chosen. All of these status' positions require certain role behaviors and are intertwined with identity formation. It is through status and role performance that identities are formed.

Identity

Stryker and Burke[26] maintain that individuals are made up of many different selves which are a result of the groups and organizations in which these individuals participate and interact. As individuals interact in any given situation, they take on the role identity that will best accommodate the event or situation. Stryker and Burke define the concept of identity as:

> persons have as many identities as distinct networks of relationships in which they occupy positions and play roles. In identity theory usage, social roles are expectations attached to positions occupied in network relationships; identities are internalized role expectations.[27]

Role identities are two pronged: a role is external and is connected to social position and the agreed upon ways of knowing of any group, organization, or society. Identity is internal in which meanings and expectations are tied to the role.[28] The context for these internalized meanings and expectations are provided by the social norms and behaviors of the group.

Commitment

The connection between identity and role behavior is in the individual's commitment to an identity. Commitment is defined through two avenues interactional commitment and affective commitment.[29] Interactional commitment is a component of the external depth and breadth of the relationships associated with any give identity.[30] This means that the greater the number of social relationships derived from an identity the greater the commitment to that identity. Secondly, affective commitment is related to the internal emotional ties an individual has to any given identity.[31] This suggests that the greater the emotional attachment to an identity the greater the commitment to that identity.[32] Therefore, an individual's attachment or commitment to an identity is determined by the scope of the relationships and the emotional ties to those relationships. In short, the extent of commitment to an identity is determined through a mixture of variables including time spent with the identity, routine use of an identity and the density of the ties an individual has with the identity. This degree of commitment will establish the salience of the identity.

Salience

The concept of salience is related to identity and role behavior. Salience refers to the hierarchy of identities within an individual's status set "portfolio" (e.g., parent, worker, buyer, homeowner, student, daughter, wife, husband, son, and boss). Stryker and Burke define salience as "the probability that an identity will be invoked across a variety of situations, or alternatively across persons in a given situation."[33] Identity theorists maintain that the more comfortable (not necessarily more pleased with the role) an individual is with an identity the more likely that identity will have a higher ranking within the hierarchy of their identity portfolio. In fact, Stryker and Burke describe the salience principle in this way:

the higher the salience of an identity relative to other identities incor-
porated into the self, the greater the probability of behavioral choices
in accord with the expectations attached to that identity.[34]

Simply, individuals have identities, whether intentional or unintentional,
likeable or not likeable, such as the identity of mother, professor, friend, Black
Sheep member, son, daughter, worker, customer and each of these identities
have an expected role behavior that is common to each identity. All individuals
have many varied identities they utilize in any given day, and more often than
not, these identities overlap. However, in relation to salience it is the potential of
a specific identity to be evoked rather than the number or variance of identities.

An example of identity salience is thinking about identities as clothes in a
wardrobe. The clothes an individual is more comfortable wearing will most likely be the clothes they most often take out of the closet to wear. It is the clothes
that are in the back of the closet that have less "salience." However, the clothes
(i.e. identity) in the back of the closet may not actually be less desirable than the
clothes (i.e. identity) in the front of the closet but more of a function of internal
and external commitment. An individual may want to wear the clothes (identity)
in the back of the closet but the affective attachment is limited by the opportunity to perform the role. The concept of salience is tied to the commitment (interactional and affective attachment) to an identity more than an aspiration to
any particular identity. Thus salience is a component of commitment. However,
individuals can commit to an aspired identity through machinations of their own
in regard to finding opportunities to perform a role; therefore an individual develops a stronger commitment to an identity through routine use.

Self-Knowledge

McCall and Simmons in their work, *Identities and Interactions*, maintain that
"role identities themselves are not equally important to the individual but differ
in their prominence."[35] Moreover, Stryker and Serpe suggest that prominence is
not as tied to the amount of time within an identity as it is to an individual's
emotional attachment to an identity.[36] In other words, while time spent within an
identity has its importance in regard to how committed an individual is to an
identity, it does not determine entirely the individual's emotional or affective
attachment to the role behavior. The individual's emotional or affective attachment to the role behavior is a reflection of how the individual views themselves.
This is where the concept of self-knowledge becomes significant for identity
construction and maintenance. Self-knowledge incorporates multiple selves and
allows the individual to develop, manipulate, and control to some degree one's
interpretation of self and role behavior.

Serpe discusses the construction of self-knowledge, maintaining that it is
"selective and creative, and reflects the social history, perceptions and actions of
an individual."[37] Therefore, how an individual thinks about herself or himself is

a reflection of not only their past perceptions of self, but also is a reflection of how one wants to be perceived in the future. This allows for the manipulation of how others view the individual and the individual's own interpretation of self. For my work, self-knowledge is an important element to understanding identity theory and Black Sheep members too.

Even though identities are both chosen and imposed upon by the individual, there is still room for the individual's influence in how others view him or her and how the individual views her or her or himself. In any given situation, an individual has the ability to view her or himself and make adjustments to their role performance. Identity theorists refer to this as cognition.[38] Cognition relates to the ability to think about and consider a role. In addition to thinking about a role and making adjustments to the role performance, Serpe contends that the whole thinking and manipulating process will affect not only the identity in question but also other identities.[39] Furthermore, Serpe maintains that "It is unlikely that spending time thinking or planning about activities related to one's identity does not have either an explicit or implicit impact on other identities."[40] This is because each different identity will affect each other across situations and time.

In sum, identity theory therefore draws from symbolic interaction, specifically from the works of Mead and Blumer. Identity theory applies Mead's understanding of self and the generalized other and how individuals manipulate their role performance in relation to how they view their role performance and in relation to how they perceive others view their role performance. The insights drawn from Blumer are within his conceptualization and modification of Thomas' "definition of the situation" in which three basic premises are prominent. The first is that meaning is subjective and individuals and groups respond to things in relation to their subjective meaning; it is not always static. Secondly, Blumer maintains that the meaning of an action or event for a person is a reaction to the individual's interpretation of how others view her or him. Briefly, this means individuals define meaning to action or events in relation to how they believe they are perceived. Blumer's third premise focuses on meaning as a result of group or individual interpretations of a situation or event. All three of these premises are seen by Blumer as constantly changing in accordance to more interpretation.

In summary, identity theorists expanded the symbolic interactionist theories to incorporate the concepts of identity, commitment, identity salience, and self-knowledge. These theorists maintain that individuals have many identities and within all of these identities are role behavior expectations; the extent to which an identity exists or to what degree is determined by interactional and affective attachment. Identity salience refers to the probability that an identity will be invoked at any given situation or across situations and self-knowledge is described as the ability that an individual has to interpret and manipulate their role performance.

Identity Theory and the Christian Biker

Identity theory will provide the framework used to further understand the behaviors and motivations of the members of the Black Sheep Harley-Davidson for Christ Motorcycle Ministry. This theoretical framework will provide insight as to how an individual develops and maintains the identities of the Christian, biker, Christian biker and Black Sheep member by specifically utilizing the theoretical concepts of identity, commitment, identity salience, and self-knowledge. Another worthy reason for grounding this project in symbolic interaction theory is the emphasis it places on naturalistic, empirical research. This research approach complements ethnography in which the researcher submerges her-or-himself into the natural flow of social life as it happens.

As the general public becomes more aware of the biker subculture (through media and marketing, for example) biker identity has become more desirable. As desirability increases, individuals develop ways to mold themselves to fit the biker identity, taking the steps necessary to become part of the larger biker group. As the individual becomes more grounded in the subculture, they will attempt to master the biker role and role behavior. In regard to the Christian biker, specifically the Black Sheep HDFC bikers, they merge the identities of Christian and biker through membership in the Black Sheep Harley-Davidsons for Christ Motorcycle Ministry. Of particular interest to my research is determining which identity was established first, the biker or the Christian. For example, was the individual a Christian who wanted to be a biker, or was the individual a biker that wanted to be a Christian? Also of interest, is how the respondents learned the role behavior/expectations to perform the roles (biker, Christian and Christian biker).

This work explores both the biker identity and the Christian identity of the members of the Black Sheep Harley-Davidson for Christ Motorcycle Ministry. This research first attempts to ascertain whether the individuals in question were Christians first or bikers first. The next area of interest is how the individual identifies her-or-himself: as a biker, a Christian, or a Christian biker and what kind of meanings these identities have for the individual. Another area of interest is how these roles and role behaviors converge and diverge over time and across situations and if the individuals recognize the distinction within and outside the roles. Finally, my work explores which role derives more commitment: the Christian or the biker.

When and how a member of Black Sheep HDFC activates the Christian biker role is determined by the amount of time spent within the group, the strengths of the networks, and the emotional ties to both the identity and the other members of the Black Sheep HDFC, i.e. commitment. Black Sheep HDFC members receive strong support for the identity when the group is riding together, participating in meetings, and attending biker events. Other symbols equal in value for supporting the biker identity is the Black Sheep patch, the Harley-Davidson motorcycle, all the Harley-Davidson accessories, the marketing and advertising techniques of the Harley-Davidson Corporation that romanticize the Harley-Davidson rider, and the extensive media coverage.

While the biker identity is more prominent to the veteran biker it may not have the greatest importance because the role and its expected behavior are already firmly established. This is not the case for new bikers who are trying to establish themselves into the subculture of the biker community. Identity theory, specifically commitment, states the more time one spends within the biker community the stronger the ties are to that community. The stronger commitment or higher in salience an identity becomes, the greater the probability the identity will summon behavioral choices common to the biker identity. Therefore, the more time spent with bikers, the more likely the behavior of the biker will be evoked.

The members of Black Sheep HDFC who have long histories of riding motorcycles have developed more networks and greater emotional ties to the identity than the newer, less-experienced members. Therefore, the social norms and values are less known or the role behavior is, at least, not as easily portrayed for the newer members. Therefore, the degree of activeness within the group will have a strong effect on the ability of the newer members to perform the role. The activities are a vehicle for new bikers to develop their role identity as biker. The more time an individual spends within the biker community, the more comfortable the person will become with the role behavior. While the degree of emotional or affective attachment may be the same for both the veteran biker and the newer less-experienced biker, the ability to successfully perform the role should, in fact, be easier for the veteran biker. The more comfortable the individual becomes with the role behavior the less likely they will feel it necessary to have their role behavior confirmed by other bikers within the community.

My research findings suggest that Black Sheep members are more closely tied to their relationship with God than with their relationship with their bikes. This, of course, is not consistent with other Harley-Davidson motorcycle groups. Findings also demonstrate that not all members of Black Sheep are actively engaged in bringing "Jesus to the Street." While most members are fairly active within the group they all differentiate in regard to their Christian convictions. This could, however, be a result of some members being more devoted Christians than the other members. Furthermore, the dual roles (Christian and biker) played by Black Sheep members differentiate in regard to Christian "maturity." Some members will actually down play the role of Christian in certain social contexts and play up the role of biker, while other members will identify as Christians first and foremost. Most interesting, however, is that many of the members of Black Sheep have identified themselves as "different," "outside the loop" or as Black Sheep prior to their conversion to Christianity. In fact, this research has found that most members literally feel like "Black Sheep" even within the traditional Christian environment and use the Black Sheep Motorcycle Ministry in place of the more traditional Christian environment.

Notes

1. Wallace and Wolf, 1999.

2. Thompson and Hickey, 2002.

3. Thompson and Hickey, 2002.

4. Thomas and Thomas, 572; Collins 1988, 1994.

5. Lemert, 1953; Goffman 1961; Becker, 1963; Scheff, 1966; Mercer, 1973.

6. Collins, 1988.

7. Cooley, 1902.

8. Mead, 1934; 1938.

9. Mead; 1938.

10. Blumer, 2.

11. Collins, 268.

12. Blumer, 4.

13. Blumer, 5.

14. Collins, 1984, 1988.

15. Collins, 1984, 1988.

16. Collins, 1984, 1988.

17 Stets and Burke, 2000a.

18. Stets and Burke, 2000a

19. Serpe, 1987 , 1991; Stryker and Serpe, 1994: Stryker and Burke, 2000.

20. Stets and Burke, 2002b.

21. Stets and Burke, 2002b.

22. Cooley, 1902.

23. Stets and Burke 2002b.

24. Stryker and Serpe, 1994 16.

25. Serpe 1991 58.

26. Stryker and Burke, 2000.

27. Stryker and Burke, 2000 287.

28. Stryker and Burke, 2002.

29. Serpe, 1987; Serpe and Stryker, 1987; Stryker, 1987.

30. Serpe, 1987; Serpe and Stryker, 1987; Stryker, 1987.

31. Serpe, 1987; Serpe and Stryker, 1987; Stryker, 1987.

32. Serpe, 1987; Serpe and Stryker, 1987; Stryker, 1987.

33. Stryker and Burke, 2000: 286.

34. Stryker and Burke, 2000: 286.

35. McCall and Simmons 1978: 80.

36. Stryker and Serpe 1994.

37. Serpe 1991: 56.

38. Serpe 1987, 1991; Stryker and Serpe, 1994; Stryker and Burke 2000

39. Serpe 1991

40. Serpe, 1991: 60.

CHAPTER THREE

Methodology/Analysis

This project is an ethnography in which the subculture of Black Sheep Harley-Davidson for Christ (Black Sheep HDFC) is studied. I utilize the methodological approach known as participant observation. Ethnography is the portrayal of a culture and is, among other things, both exploratory and descriptive in design. "An ethnography represents a detailed study of the life and activities of a group of people" and typically relies on first hand observation.[1]

Ethnographical research uses the technique of participant observation which is defined as "a research method by which investigators systematically observe people while joining in their routine activities."[2] Participant observation is historically tied to field research and is common within the field of Anthropology. Ideally, this methodological approach allows the researcher to participate in the everyday life of the people the researcher is studying. Lofland and Lofland maintain in their work on qualitative research that the basic principles of participant observation theory are:

> 1) that face-to-face interaction is the fullest condition of participating in the mind of another human being, and 2) that you must participate in the mind of another human being (in sociological terms, "take the role of the other") to acquire social knowledge.[3]

The benefits of this approach are obvious in regard to access and personal knowledge or gaining an "insider's look" of the people or group being studied. The advantages of doing ethnographical research lie in the richness and intimacy of describing and analyzing any given group or event through direct experience. The qualitative approach allows the unique nuances of the group or event being studied to come to life. This approach often provides insights that would otherwise be either missed or ignored by other research methods such as surveys or experiments commonly found within quantitative research epistemologies. Ethnographies provide a natural setting for the researcher to work and permits human face-to-face contact for the purpose of developing an intimate understanding of the culture or group. In general, most of the data collected using participant observation is derived through informal interviews and augmented and supported with observation.[4] However, traditional participant observation embraces a combination of listening, watching and questioning. All of these skills are crucial to a successful research project.[5]

To completely appreciate the strengths of the ethnographical approach the researcher must maintain flexibility and allow the rich research data to speak for itself. It is understood that the data is often only as good as its researcher, yet I feel, however, the subjects and subculture I am studying, in this case the Black Sheep HDFC Motorcycle Ministry, must represent its own voice and I, as the researcher, only the vehicle in which to tell their story. Often problematic in any research is the researcher's enthusiasm to support hypotheses and expectations and as a result the richness of the data is lost. To give life to the data as it represented itself to me, I covered all the questions on the interview schedule but allowed my respondents to speak freely about all aspects of their membership in Black Sheep Harley-Davidsons for Christ Motorcycle.

The downfalls of this approach are also obvious in regard to the necessity of the researcher to develop a balance between the role of participant observer and researcher. The ethnographical researcher can suffer from a lack of objectivity and distance which can contaminate the data. Another problem with the ethnography is the focus on one group or one culture limiting the finding's generalizability. Nonetheless, Feagin, Orum, and Sjoberg contend that ethnographies have been very valuable in the origination of new ideas and theories in the social sciences.[6] If the following research does not lend itself to represent all Christian bikers, this does not diminish the value of the research or limit its validity. Ethnographies have both their strengths and weaknesses, however, qualitative research, in particular case studies, are descriptive and insightful to social science research.

Drawing on these insights and given the lack of available literature on motorcycle ministries, I have developed an exploratory research design and adopted two methodological strategies. First, I interviewed fifteen members of the Black Sheep HDFC including the founder and national president, chapter presidents, chapter historian, and various members to ascertain information regarding Black Sheep HDFC and the individual members. Second, I draw on my own experience within the ministry itself.

I am and have been actively involved with the Black Sheep since January of 2000, shortly after its birth in November 1999. Therefore, I am familiar with the habits, cultural norms, values, and behaviors of the people within this particular motorcycle ministry and for that matter through association I am also familiar, or at least aware, with the ways of other Christian motorcycle groups. Due to my active participation in this group, I have been able to build a trust and develop a rapport with most of the members of this ministry. Consequently, some of the data presented is drawn from experiences and knowledge realized through this participation.

Moreover, I have also been actively involved with the biker subculture since 1975; this association with the biker subculture provides me with knowledge of the social norms, behaviors, and vernacular of the subculture as a whole. Furthermore, I have published work on the saloon society biker subculture "Women Who Ride Harleys"[7] and my master's thesis, titled "Obscene but not Heard," was also on the saloon society biker subculture (any conclusions drawn from this personal experience will be noted).

Due to the nature of the ethnography, the members that are most active represent the general population studied. However, crucial to understanding the group as a whole and the motivations of the active members will be to understand the motivations of the non-active members as well, therefore, I have included non-active member interviews. The interview schedule covered information regarding not only the machinations of the group, but also the individual motivations of those interviewed in regard to what the ministry/group provides to the interviewee both spiritually and non-spiritually. The strength of utilizing an interview format is in its face-to-face interaction with the respondent.[8] Utilizing face-to-face interviews allows for open-ended questions that often lead to additional questions to help the researcher fully understand the respondent's answers and motivations.[9] The weakness of the face-to-face interview format is in its lack of consistency, while there is focus on asking the questions in the same way with each respondent it is not always possible, causing a problem with reliability.[10] Furthermore, the face-to-face interview approach is time consuming and relies on the benevolence of the interviewees to give the researcher their time and energy.

The interview process with each individual (fifteen subjects, four females and eleven males) averaged approximately one hour in length. The population studied was members of the Black Sheep HDFC. The sample of individual interviews was drawn from active and inactive members. The interviews were manually recorded and recorded by a court reporter using a computer aided transcription (CAT) process. The CAT process consists of the stenographer copying down the words spoken by the interviewer and interviewee. The stenograph machine is hooked by cable to a laptop computer with a software program that translates the stenotype into English. The accuracy rate is one hundred percent after correction. The correction is necessary because the computer dictionary does not always include all the words used by the interviewer and interviewee in the interview. A copy of the interview is immediately given to the researcher after each interview on a 3 ½" floppy disk. The presentation of the interview on the disk is in Microsoft Word. The opportunity to use a court reporter became available to me through another member of the Black Sheep Motorcycle Ministry. The benefits of using the court reporter are many and include the opportunity to maintain eye contact with the subjects allowing the researcher to note facial expressions, speed in both the interview and also transcription, the option to ask questions when answers to questions beg additional questions, accuracy, and a host of other benefits not yet realized. One drawback may include the possible discomfort of having another person listening to the interview. However, the same problem may exist with an audiotape recorder or videotape recorder.

In addition to oral testimonies, I have collected paraphernalia that is representative of this group including: patches, clothing, meeting agenda handouts, pictures, video tape, and any and all additional tangible information that pertains to the Black Sheep HDFC. Furthermore, included in my work is the description and evaluation of the various events attended by the Black Sheep Motorcycle Ministry.

The following chapters will attempt to support the theoretical framework provided above. Chapter four will describe and discuss Black Sheep HDFC's organization, history, mission, and activities. Chapter five will describe who the Black Sheep HDFC members are including where they were raised, childhood family life, gender, age, race, occupations, current family situations, and length of membership in Black Sheep HDFC. Chapter Six will examine biker and Christian identities. Chapter Seven, the final chapter, will encompass the conclusion and findings.

Notes

1. Feagin, Orum, and Sjoberg, 1991: 4.
2. Macionis, 2001: 43.
3. Lofland and Lofland, 1991: 18.
4. Lofland and Lofland, 1991.
5. Lofland and Lofland, 1995.
6. Feagin, Orum, and Sjoberg
7. Anderson-Facile 1994.
8. Babbie, 1992.
9. Babbie, 1992.
10. Babbie, 1992.

CHAPTER FOUR

Black Sheep: The Organization

While it is most likely that Christians have been riding motorcycles since the late 1800s, when motorcycles were first produced, it was not until 1975 that the first organized Christian motorcycle club was established. Herb Shreve founded the Christian Motorcycle Association (CMA), a non-denominational ministry for the purpose of evangelism, which now boasts 55,000 members and 400 chapters.[1] Since this time many other Christian Motorcycle Organizations have been established. Black Sheep Harley-Davidsons for Christ Motorcycle Ministry began in late1999 with the sole purpose of ministering to the Harley Owners Group (HOG). Unique to the Black Sheep HDFC Motorcycle Ministry is not only its focus on HOG, but also members must own and ride Harley-Davidson motorcycles. This chapter will profile the Black Sheep Harley-Davidsons for Christ Motorcycle Ministry including a description of its inception in late 1999 and an historical trajectory of the ministry's growth, the groups structural organization, the ministry's mission statement, and finally, the activities and mission work of the group.

History

Pertinent to understanding the birthing of the Black Sheep Harley-Davidsons for Christ Motorcycle Ministry is to recognize the motivations behind the founders and founding officers. The founding officers were the individuals that fashioned the name of Black Sheep HDFC and formed the beginnings of the organization. While there were only five men that rode together and decided to form a ministry called the Black Sheep, the explosive growth is the work of many. The national president and founder of the Black Sheep Harley-Davidsons for Christ, Pastor Marty Edwards, started the ministry serendipitously. He had not planned to begin a ministry using his motorcycle as a venue to minister to motorcycle riders. He had actually bought a motorcycle for sport. Shortly, after purchasing the motorcycle Marty Edwards realized that many people he knew also rode, so a group of men started riding together. Seemingly Black Sheep HDFC was not a planned project, in fact, it grew from a group of Christian men going on rides together and eating meals together talking about their love of riding. When questioned about the conceptual birthing of the Black Sheep HDFC, Marty Edwards maintained:

> I didn't mean to. I did not buy the motorcycle to use it for ministry. It just sort of happened. I met half dozen Christian riders, and we started riding together and realized there was an opportunity to use motorcycles to share the Lord. At some point, we decided to formalize our relationship. I suppose, would be the birth of Black Sheep. There were five members and motorcycles. Yeah, so we started with five members. And then we would meet people on H.O.G. rides. Other people in the church, we found out, had Harleys in their garage underneath a blanket, so they started riding with us. Other people went out and bought Harleys to be a part of this.

However, there is more to this than it "just sort of happened" and it stems from Marty's career pattern and unique personality. He describes his career history in this way:

> I am radical ... and of course, that's a relative term—but I am serious about my walk with Christ. I have tried to understand and reconcile the Word of God to the way Christians live. Yet, several times in my Christian walk, I have become frustrated, not with God, but with God's people. We say one thing and we do another. I think they call that hypocrisy. So, I have left the church—from the professional aspect of the church—several times in my ministry.

At the time Black Sheep HDFC was just forming Marty Edwards was the senior pastor of Lambs Fellowship Church, a Free Methodist denomination, in Murrieta, California. He had been the senior pastor of this church from 1987 until 2001, when he stepped down from his leadership position to consider other career opportunities. Marty believed that he was no longer effective as a preacher within this particular church and wanted something more.

> In thirteen years, we planted four churches. Three survived. And there are hundreds of people that have come to Christ and all the good things that happen with a church. However, I found myself a bit at odds with the people of the church and found them self-involved, hedonistic. The church became about them again. And in my efforts to encourage the church to reach out, to share their faith with friends and neighbors, I found myself transitioning from a fairly articulate communicator to a nag. So here I am a pastor trying to motivate the church to get involved with the community. Finding most people are reluctant to do that. Meantime, on Mondays, I'm riding my motorcycle.

Marty Edwards is not what one would expect of a pastor. He is of average height and chubby, with a shaved head, pierced ears, and tattoos. In short, Marty Edwards does not look like a pastor. Nor does he act like a traditional pastor; his background is not traditional either. Marty Edwards did not graduate from high school, yet through the help of others, he did receive a BA degree in Christian education and youth ministry from Point Loma Nazarene University. Later he received his MA degree in cross-cultural studies from Fullerton Theological Seminary. Marty Edwards was coloring outside the lines for the better part of his career and the Black Sheep Harley-Davidsons for Christ Motorcycle Ministry is just another example his non-traditional approach to Christian ministry.

Marty describes his early days in ministry as unconventional. He noticed that while he was a Christian, his approach to evangelism differed from the traditional forms of Christianity. He began his career as a youth pastor, but that did not work out because "I not only had a commitment to the kids of the church, but to the kids in the street. But found more often than not Christian parents didn't want their kids to be associated with kid's ministry." At this point, Marty found that he did not blend with the traditional church and felt because he "colored outside the lines" this was "difficult for the church to reconcile. I became a little odd for them." So he started a Christian rock band and used that as a means to reach out to kids in the street. For three years, he traveled with this band "who would play everything from prisons to coffee houses to street concerts to whatever...college campuses." When he stopped playing and traveling with the band he tried other youth pastor positions, but again found that he was not what the traditional church wanted. It was at this point, he planted the Lambs Fellowship Free Methodist Church in Murrieta, California. Thirteen years later, he bought a motorcycle and started riding his bike around town. Shortly after the purchase of his motorcycle he realized that he wanted to do something different. "I was frustrated. I was driving the church rather than leading the church and realized I was no longer the best thing for the church. And I resigned."

Marty had not planned to start a Christian motorcycle ministry, it was just part of who he is and how he works. What makes Marty's evangelism unique to the ways of the traditional church is his desire to "take Jesus to the streets."

> What attracted me about Black Sheep was, once again, taking Jesus from the church to the streets. Jesus, if you look at his ministry, he only had three years of ministry. He taught in the synagogue. But the greater majority of his ministry took place in the street where the people were. Likewise, Black Sheep starts with church people and is still committed to the local church, but is absolutely committed to reaching the lost in the streets.

The name Black Sheep also came about by accident. This was given to them by the people that saw them riding together as a group. The formal name Black Sheep came from bystanders. However, their identity as a group was just in its beginning stages.

When we started riding and identifying ourselves as a group, people would say "you must be the black sheep of the flock," going back to Lamb's Fellowship. The name stuck. And it was justified because, throughout New Testament Scripture, the church is referred to by names like "alien," "outcast," "foreigner," "not of this world." So "Black Sheep" is a euphemism that means exactly what the Bible says a Christian is the oddball, the outcast, the different one. And we are called to come out from among the world and to be different. So Black Sheep, the name, stuck because it fits.

Black Sheep HDFC Motorcycle Ministry now has a membership of over five hundred men and women. One of the reasons their membership has grown so quickly in the last five and a half years is due to ABC World News Tonight report about the ministry. In December 2002, ABC World News Tonight with Peter Jennings did a special on the Black Sheep HDFC Motorcycle Ministry. This special was broadcast nationwide and the ministry went from having members in five states to members in ten states within about sixty days.

The Black Sheep Harley-Davidsons for Christ's website defines what and who the group is and what they do. It informs about upcoming events, includes pictures and information about the National ministry as well as the individual chapters. The website also has the following statement from Marty Edwards:

Greetings to you in the name of our Lord Jesus Christ!
After 30 years of ministry in the local church, Christ has called me to rally the tens of thousands of Harley riders whose lives have been committed to Christ, to organize and strategically reach out to other riders with the Good News and compassion of Jesus Christ.
Black Sheep Harley-Davidsons for Christ, was born out of passion and vision to bring the Gospel to those who ride. With so many similar clubs and ministries doing such a good job, it was our specific burden to focus our ministry on H.O.G. (Harley Owners Group) members. They (We) are a breed unto themselves, who often keep to themselves, allowing only other H.O.G. members to speak into their lives. Such a focus should not be viewed as exclusive (for all are welcome to Christ's love) but rather strategic! Though we often find ourselves ministering to other riders, outlaws and those who don't ride a motorcycle at all, it is to the 500,000 + H.O.G. members to whom we have been called.
Black Sheep is not only H.O.G. focused but family oriented. We are pleased to ride as single adults, married couples and often with our children. Whole families attend our events and rides, sometimes even in a car!
Our vision is nationwide. While our headquarters are stationed in Southern California, we have growing chapters and pre-chapters (members at large) throughout the Midwest and East.
We do not 'LIVE TO RIDE' or 'RIDE TO LIVE!' We live and ride for Jesus Christ and we are ready to die for Him!
If I can ever answer any of your questions about our ministry, please do not hesitate to call me at (951) 757-9008 or email me at slow-dog@blacksheepHDFC.org.

May the Lord richly bless you and keep you safe as you ride!
Marty 'Slow Dog' Edwards Founder/National President

In late 1999, Black Sheep Harley-Davidsons for Christ Motorcycle Ministry started with five people who rode their motorcycles together for fun and turned their fun into a ministry called the "Black Sheep Harley-Davidsons for Christ. By 2005 the Black Sheep HDFC motorcycle ministry" increased from five members to over five hundred members, currently with twenty-seven chapters, representing seventeen states.

Organization

Black Sheep Harley-Davidsons for Christ Motorcycle Ministry is made up of a National Headquarters, twenty-seven chapters, and many members. Not all members belong to a chapter, because organized chapters are not available in every area. The Black Sheep special on ABC World News Tonight brought forth many new members in areas where there are no chapters. Marty Edwards travels to these different areas once there is enough interest to start a chapter and assists in the beginning stages of each new chapter.

Marty Edwards views himself as an "administrative overseer" of the Black Sheep HDFC Motorcycle Ministry. "Each chapter is bound by a statement of faith and a set of bylaws. And my job is to try to keep us going in that direction." Marty Edwards, as National President, presides over the entire ministry. He also writes and produces a national newsletter which is sent out to members and non-members (any person that asks to be on the mailing list). Marty sends Black Sheep newsletters out worldwide including to Saudi Arabia, Kuwait, and Indonesia. However, there are no actual members outside the United States.

The national organization also has a board of directors to assist in the overseeing of the ministry. Marty Edwards is the national president, there are also two vice presidents, two secretaries, and one treasurer. This group monitors the organization as a whole and controls the funding. Funding for the Black Sheep HDFC Motorcycle Ministry comes from local churches, the Free Methodist Church of North America, and member financial support. All national and local officers, with the exception of Marty Edwards, are on a voluntary basis and no compensation is received for these positions.

Each chapter consists of an elected president, elected vice president, elected treasurer, elected secretary, appointed historian, appointed road captains, appointed safety director and a Chaplain. The elected posts are for one year.

New chapters can be added at anytime as long as the new chapters adhere to the following rules:

1. A new chapter may be organized when four or more officers are present and committed, serving for at least one year as president, vice president, secretary and treasurer.
2. A new chapter must be approved at the National level.

3. A new chapter may not alter the club patch, our values, bylaws, etc.

4. A new chapter may operate their own newsletter publication separate from the national newsletter.

5. A new chapter may operate fundraisers for their own purposes, but may not print their own tee shirts, stickers, pins, or any other things using the Black Sheep name or logos.

6. It is strongly suggested that each chapter secure a chase vehicle and trailer to be used on long runs and the purpose of ministry to others.[2]

In addition to the by-laws for the chapters there are general rules that are to be followed to by each and every member. When a member joins the Black Sheep HDFC Motorcycle Ministry they sign a contract agreeing to the following prerequisites and rules:

Prerequisites for Membership
1. Must be an active member/attendee of a local Christian Church evidencing their submission to Biblical authority.
2. Must complete a membership application and include all fees as well as a pastoral recommendation.
3. Must own and operate a Harley-Davidson motorcycle (or an American-made v-twin cruiser whose engine is based upon the Harley-Davidson motor design) or be the owner's spouse and passenger.

If a prospective member is able to fulfill the prerequisites they must also accept and follow the general rules of the group which include:

General Rules
1. Black Sheep members may belong to other motorcycle clubs as long as: additional clubs are not in conflict with the mission and values of Black Sheep HDFC (see mission statement and values below).
2. The Black Sheep colors are the primary patch displayed on the back.
3. Alcoholic beverages will not be consumed on any club rides or functions.
4. Violence will not be indicative of our members.
5. Vulgar language will not be indicative of our members.
6. Members will restrict themselves from becoming involved in activities of a sexual, promiscuous or flirtatious nature.
7. Members will not wear or display anything dishonoring to Christ (i.e. t-shirts, pins, etc.).
8. Members will always conduct themselves in a manner worthy of their calling in Christ.
9. The intent of these rules is not meant to be exhaustive, but to clarify what some Christians may consider "gray" areas. It is not the intent of this club to become sectarian or legalistic in regards to Christian character. We simply want to represent Christ well in an otherwise ungodly world. Any specific decisions may be settled by the local or national chapter leader.[3]

This organization has both a national organizational structure and a chapter organizational structure with rules and regulations that must be followed if one wants to maintain membership.

Patch

Another aspect of the club is the "club colors" or patch which is a combination of browns, shades of gold, and black. Colors can only be worn by members of the club that have met the prerequisites and agreed to the rules of the club. All colors/patches need to be worn to all club functions. The rules also state that "colors will not be defended with violence and unlike, some clubs, Black Sheep makes no distinction between males and females with respect to colors being worn."[4] Furthermore, "the colors/patch remain the property of the local chapter and must be surrendered by any member leaving the club or any reason."[5]

In the five and half years that Black Sheep HDFC has been in existence a few members have sold their bikes and have therefore returned their patches. In a couple of cases members have been asked to relinquish their patch due to the member not following the rules of the ministry.

Mission

The mission statement of the Black Sheep HDFC Motorcycle ministry is to "Know Him and Make Him Known." Formally the statement is as follows:

> The ministry of Black Sheep Harley-Davidson for Christ exists to introduce Jesus Christ to the world of motorcycle riders, for the purpose of making more and better disciples through the ministry of the local church Black Sheep's primary focus is to HOG (Harley Owners Group). Such a focus should not be seen as exclusive, but rather as strategic.[6]

In the interview with the national president, Marty Edwards, he defined and discussed the mission statement of Black Sheep in this way:

> The mission of Black Sheep is to make Christ known to the motorcycle world and then to introduce those people to the local church. And that's more ministry and more responsibility than some people want to own. This is a wonderful, wonderful group of people who have all the makings of a church. They are just missing the spiritual aspect of God.

In addition, to the mission statement the Black Sheep HDFC Motorcycle Ministry also has a section on their web page that is referred to as "our values." This list is related to the mission statement.

VALUES OF THE ORGANIZATION
Our Values
1. We value our personal relationship with Jesus Christ.
2. We value the Bible as our sole authority for living.
3. We value relationships with brothers and sisters in the local church.
4. We value relationships with brothers and sisters in the motorcycle community.
5. We value deeply those who have yet to receive the Gospel of Jesus Christ.
6. We value being IN the world but not OF the world.
7. We value our government and its laws and so we obey them with enthusiasm
8. We value our lives and our families and so we ride safe.[7]

To become a member of the Black Sheep HDFC Motorcycle Ministry a prospective member must be a practicing Christian, agree and adhere to the by-laws, mission statement, values, general rule, and patch rules.

Black Sheep Club Activities

Black Sheep Motorcycle Ministry maintains that an important part of the ministry is providing service to the local community. They claim that they want to do "street ministry" therefore one would expect that the organization would be actively pursuing ongoing opportunities to serve. Yet to be effective in ministry and to develop group solidarity there needs to be group activities that help build up the body of Black Sheep HDFC Motorcycle Ministry. The following will outline the club activities of the Black Sheep HDFC Motorcycle Ministry.

Most Black Sheep activities and mission work are family oriented and children are encouraged to be active within the group although, they cannot join Black Sheep HDFC until they are at least eighteen years old and own a Harley-Davidson motorcycle. The ministry is motivated to be a family oriented ministry group. This is a reasonable motivation considering many of the members have children or grandchildren under the age of eighteen years.

Meetings

The first Saturday morning of each month there is a roving national meeting held in a restaurant in Southern, California. At one time the national meeting was held only in Temecula, California but due to the increase in members and chapters the meetings are now held in a different Southern California location each month. These meetings are open to members and non-members. Often these meetings are attended by other motorcycle ministries such as the Servants for Christ and people that have either been invited to the meeting by a member or have found out about the meeting in another way. The meeting covers issues concerning the group as a whole including upcoming events, reports on previous events, illnesses/accidents of members or H.O.G. members, introduction of new members and chapters, news important to the whole group, and any other information that is pertinent. The national meeting is also a place for fellowship, encouragement, and fun. There are contests and biker paraphernalia is raffled off. There is often a biblical message given by Marty Edwards. There is generally around one hundred and sixty members attending the meetings, but there have been as many as two hundred and twenty members that attend this breakfast meeting. The meetings last approximately two hours and are followed by a group ride. The ride location is determined in advance, so members who are able to ride that morning can decide if they are interested in joining the group ride.

In addition to national meetings, each chapter has their own chapter meetings which are most often held on Saturday mornings. These meetings are similar to the national meetings, but the information pertains to the local chapter. They are open to any person interested in attending the meeting; they need not be a member. Unique to the local chapter meetings is the induction of new members. These meetings are also followed by a group ride. Members from other chapters often attend other chapter meetings to show support and to be part of the ride.

Moreover, there is a West Coast Rally (the first year it was called the National Rally) held each year. So far the rallies have all been held California, generally a place half way between Northern California and Southern California. This meeting provides an opportunity for all Black Sheep HDFC members to meet each other and find out what other chapters are doing. The three day rally begins on Friday and ends on Sunday. On Friday and Saturday nights the whole group worships and prays together. They listen to guest speakers, hold raffles and socialize. During the day there are various rides planned so a member has a choice of where he or she wants to ride. Often times a chase vehicle will follow the group on the day rides, so the children can be included (a chase vehicle is a vehicle and trailer that follows the group on long rides, and sometimes short rides, in case of an emergency. The trailer is available to haul bikes and the vehicle is useful for hauling extra people at the national rally). A car trip is often planned for people who are tired of riding on the motorcycle or because getting to some places is not conducive to motorcycles (the rest of the time at the rallies is for eating and socializing with other members).

Since Black Sheep HDFC Motorcycle Ministry began two members have died. The first member that died was a man of seventy years named Doug who was killed while riding his motorcycle. Doug did not have a lot of experience riding and took a curve to fast and rode into incoming traffic and was killed instantly. He had only been a member of Black Sheep for about six weeks, but was well known throughout the group. The funeral was held in Temecula and about thirty Black Sheep members attended the funeral on their bikes and flying their patch.

Another member of Black Sheep died of kidney failure. John had been a member of Black Sheep HDFC for a couple of years and had held the position of vice president of the Temecula chapter. John was well known and well loved.

He had been hospitalized for approximately one month before he died. During that month there was at least one Black Sheep member at the hospital daily and some days up to thirty members present at any given time. When John died it was a great loss to the entire group. The national president of the Black Sheep HDFC presided over the funeral. John's wife and three young children requested that the Black Sheep members ride behind the hearse as it traveled to the cemetery. As many as forty-five bikes and approximately sixty members followed the hearse in double formation (side by side). John's own bike followed first behind the hearse ridden by a member of Black Sheep and good friend of John. It was a very powerful procession.

Black Sheep also attend funeral for other riders regardless of club or ministry affiliation. Their goal is to provide spiritual support as well as financial support. Many times Black Sheep members will organize and provide food for the gathering after the funeral. Also, a homemade quilt is given to the family. This is an important service that Black Sheep offers and is very helpful to the family of the deceased.

Black Sheep Cards

Black Sheep members also hand out "Black Sheep" cards to other Harley-Davidson riders. There are a variety of different cards. One card is a 4" x 6" postcard and on one side it has the Black Sheep logo and address and on the other side it has:

The 10 Things Every Biker Needs to Know Before They Die...

1). There is a God and He is a GREAT and AWESOME God!

2). He loves and cares about you very much! 'I know the plans I have for you'; declares the Lord, 'plans to prosper you and not to harm you, plans to give you hope and a future.'

3). God not only wants to help. God CAN and DOES bring about radical changes in people's lives. Bodies are healed! Addictions are broken! Families renewed!

4). Without God's help, you and I have no hope whatsoever.

5). That's because we are born with a spiritual disease. Call it 'sin.' Sin not only causes us to do things that hurt ourselves and others, but it is the root of what separates us from God.

6). The 'Good News' is that Jesus Christ died to pay for your sin and mine. We are forgiven for all that we have ever done if we simply accept the gift of Jesus on the cross and follow Him as our Lord and Savior! The Bible says 'all have sinned and fall short of the glory of God.' It continues 'the wages of sin is death but the gift of God is eternal life'.

7). All of this is well and good, but you need to know that 'to believe' is not to simply say, 'Yea Yea! I believe.' It means to love God with all of your heart so as to develop a relationship with Him through Jesus Christ.

8). Everybody makes a decision. Some say 'Yes to God' some say 'No.' Some 'think about it and wait too long and die without knowing Jesus. This is a tragedy! Hell is your worst nightmare! You'll never 'party' there with your friends. Nobody parties in hell!

9). You need to know that sooner or later everybody will bow before Jesus Christ. 'As surely as I live,' says the Lord, 'every knee will bow before me; every tongue will confess that Jesus Christ is LORD.' You can bow before Him now as your friend and Savior or after death as your judge.

10). Nothing is more important than your soul. Bodies are temporary, souls last forever! The Bible asks the question, 'What good is it for a man to gain the whole world, yet forfeit his soul?' Souls last for eternity man! And that's a long, long, time!

Can you honestly pray this prayer?
'God in Heaven, I confess to you that I am a sinner that needs to be saved. I am sorry for all of my sins and want to change and accept what Jesus did on the cross for me. I believe that Jesus Christ is the Son of God. I believe He died on the cross for me and rose from the dead! I want to serve and follow Him for the rest of my life. With God's help I will seek to understand and do all that He calls me to. Thank you for loving me. In Jesus' name I pray. Amen.
If you prayed these words, write Black Sheep and let us know.
May God bless you and keep you safe as you ride with Him![8]

All of the above events and meetings are ways in which the Black Sheep develop cohesiveness within the group. As members attend these functions they learn not only the norms, values, and behaviors of the group, but also they develop relationships. Furthermore, these events and meetings are ways in which the individuals and the group as a whole build and maintain the identity of the Christian biker and Black Sheep member.

While the above events have been very beneficial to the individual and group growth, and group solidarity of the Black Sheep HDFC Motorcycle Ministry there have been events that have not been as advantageous. In the interview with Marty Edwards he describes the events that were not successful.

We started off trying everything. One of the first things we tried was a biker church. It met once a month, midweek, and was not unlike a church service on Sunday mornings. There was music followed by a message. The problem was, once again, the Christians were coming and there weren't a lot of non-Christians coming. So it became just another entertainment aspect of the church. And I just had come from that and really wasn't interested in spending my time on another Christian Bible study. So we shut that down.

In conclusion, as Black Sheep has grown from a small group of men riding together for pleasure to a large group of men and women in ministry. They have found what events have worked to build group solidarity and what events have not been successful. Seemingly, the leadership of Black Sheep is of the mind that a good healthy ministry begins with a good healthy group. So, there are national and chapter meetings to build the group, both, in numbers and in agreed upon ways of knowing. Without these meetings and group events the ministry would not be able to support the development of the Christian biker identity, specifically the Black Sheep member. At these events and meetings individual members are able to learn the "right" Black Sheep behavior. While each member is an individual overall there are basic cultural norms and ways specific to the Black Sheep member. These events are a great opportunity for individual members to perfect their Black Sheep and Christian biker role performance. The more often a member attends meetings and other events and the more Black Sheep friends they make, the more comfortable they become with his or her ability to perform the Christian biker role and commit to the Black Sheep identity. Moreover, the more committed to the identity the member becomes the more active they are in the ministry resulting in greater identity salience. Inactive members are less likely to have strong commitment to the Black Sheep identity therefore reducing Black Sheep identity salience. The Christian identity is supported through the local church, but the Christian biker identity must be supported through the group membership within the Black Sheep or another Christian motorcycle group.

In addition to the club activities that support and encourage the members are the mission events that the ministry support and serve. Active participation in the various mission events also enhance a members commitment to the Christian biker role and promotes greater identity salience.

Missions

The Black Sheep HDFC Motorcycle Ministry is enthusiastically involved with a variety of biker events and mission activities. While the HOG organization is the primary mission for Black Sheep HDFC, there are many other events in which they participate. This section of the chapter will outline and describe the various events, both statewide and nationwide, in which Black Sheep are involved. Since serving HOG members is Black Sheep's primary mission this section will begin with a description and analysis of their work with the HOG members and conclude with the other events.

As stated earlier, the mission of Black Sheep HDFC Motorcycle Ministry is to serve and witness to HOG organization. Although HOG is a national organization the Black Sheep focus their attention on the local HOG chapters. For example the Temecula Valley HOG chapter is very cognizant of the desires of Black Sheep to serve and witness to their people. Therefore, they often request assistance from the Black Sheep including help with the weekly barbeque at the local motorcycle dealership, Quaid Harley-Davidson. Every Saturday Temecula Valley HOG serve, with the help of Black Sheep members, hot dogs, hamburgers, salad, and soda to anybody and everybody who comes to the Quaid Harley-Davidson dealership. All the supplies are donated by the dealership and the labor is supplied by HOG members and Black Sheep HDFC members. The food is free, but donations are accepted and go into the HOG chapter treasury.

Quaid Harley-Davidson and HOG also provide food for other activities such as the Pre-Laughlin run, poker runs, and open houses. The Black Sheep help with the serving of food to as many as one thousand bikers at these events. Again, the food is donated by the dealerships and the donations in these events are donated to a charity such as the Diabetes Foundation. At these larger events there are many Black Sheep members that volunteer. Generally, there are fifteen to twenty volunteers at any given time serving food, cleaning up, setting up, and preparing food. The relationship between the Temecula Valley HOG members and the Black Sheep appears cordial. These events are one way for Black Sheep members to practice the role of the biker and the Christian biker because they are socializing with all types of bikers. They are able to learn the ways of the Black Sheep as well as the ways of the biker. New and old Black Sheep members can pick up and practice the cultural norms of both groups.

The motorcycle enthusiasts that are served at these events seem to take the Black Sheep group in stride. From my perspective, they are neither for nor against the Black Sheep serving them. They just want their free food. They are polite, but perhaps wary, it seems as if they fear they will be preached to if they become too friendly. However, Black Sheep are a constant at these affairs, so they are becoming known as the group that serves. This is what the Black Sheep wants; this is their mission. To serve the HOG organization with the hope that people will see Christ through the actions of the Black Sheep members and want to know about their God

Another ministry that Black Sheep provides for the HOG organization is the hospital ministry. The national president, Marty Edwards, attempts to visit HOG members and other riders (regardless of affiliation) if they are in the hospital (at least within riding distance). He visits whether they are in the hospital because they have been hurt on their bike or for other reasons. Other members of Black Sheep also visit Harley riders in the hospital. They go to the hospital to visit, pray and minister to the patient. Of course, because the patient is bed-ridden it prevents the patient from walking away from the Black Sheep member, but seemingly the visit is appreciated. Furthermore, the Black Sheep HDFC provide handmade quilts for the people in the hospital. These quilts are quilts made of denim and flannel with a small Black Sheep patch on them.

The trailer ministry entails providing a trailer to haul bikes in situations such as accidents, breakdowns, illnesses and for any other reason a person would need their bike trailered. This service is available to any person who owns a bike regardless of make or model. This particular ministry has been very successful and has provided Black Sheep the chance to minister to many bikers. This is not an opportunity to preach, per say, but an opportunity to serve. Black Sheep ride in a group to most functions and are followed by a vehicle with a trailer referred to as the "chase vehicle." The trailer is used as a service to others at these events. Most Black Sheep chapters have their own trailers for this ministry.

Black Sheep provides the trailer service throughout the year at many of the events. Given that Black Sheep always has a chase vehicle, the opportunity to provide this service is readily available. At the end of the Prim, Nevada run (to be described further in this chapter) due to an illness a couple, not affiliated with the Black Sheep, needed to have their bike trailered back to the Los Angeles area. The bike was loaded on the trailer and the couple rode in the chase vehicle for the ride back to Southern California. Recently on the way home from a Laughlin Run, a couple had to load their bike on the Black Sheep trailer and ride in the truck because the wind was too strong and they were having trouble riding.

Love Ride

At the Love Ride, some Black Sheep provide this trailer service and do not ride themselves. There are anywhere from four to six vehicles and trailers for this event. The Love Ride began in 1981, at that time it was known as the Biker's Carnival, a fundraiser for the Muscular Dystrophy Association in which Harley-Davidson Corporation is one of its official corporate sponsors. The ride begins at the Glendale Harley-Davidson dealer in Glendale, California and ends fifty miles north at Castaic Lake, California. The last three years there have been approximately twenty thousand bikes involved in this event. For a sixty dollar entrance fee, riders receive food (ribs and chicken donated by Tony Roma's restaurants), a chance to win prizes, an opportunity to shop at the many vendor booths selling biker paraphernalia, a great ride, and a big party.

The Love Ride boasts that it is the largest one day ride in the world. "It is a place where everyone has a good time while making a difference in the community and the world we live in."[9] There are many Hollywood stars active in this event including Robbie Kreiger, David Crosby, Eric Burdon, Jackson Browne, Little Feat, Billy Idol, Bruce Springsteen, Dwight Yoakam, the Doobie Brothers, Sammy Hagar, Jay Leno, Peter Fonda, Sheryl Crow, and others. Jay Leno and Peter Fonda led the nineteenth annual Love Ride 2002 followed by twenty thousand bikes. This event has "raised $1.1 million to benefit the Reading by 9 literacy initiative and other charities, including the Muscular Dystrophy Association."[10]

This event is held on a Sunday in November. Black Sheep drive up and down Interstate 5 Freeway with their trailers and pick up bikes that are down for whatever reason, supply gas or minor repair. If necessary the bike is brought to the nearest Harley-Dealership for repair. Over the last five years Black Sheep has helped many riders at the Love Ride event. The Black Sheep have also provided assistance in regard to parking at this event. This event exposes Black Sheep members to an even larger group of bikers allowing the ministry greater opportunities to server and greater exposure as a ministry. It also allows members to further develop the identity of both the Christian biker and the overall biker. This event draws bikers from all walks of life and is a great opportunity for new riders to pick up the important norms and values of the biker subculture.

Parades

Black Sheep participate in many different parades in Southern California. At this parade there are approximately twenty riders and the chase van displaying the Black Sheep Harley-Davidson for Christ Motorcycle Ministry logo. These parades are very successful if getting the crowd to scream and cheer is the aim. In 2001 and 2002 at the Temecula Valley Parade, the Black Sheep truck pulled a trailer decorated with lights and filled with children. The bikes circled around the truck and trailer. Other chapters are also involved with riding in parades. This is an excellent opportunity to advertise for Black Sheep Harley-Davidsons for Christ Motorcycle Ministry.

Primm, Nevada Event

The Primm, Nevada bike event is sponsored by Choir Boys, a non-profit organization of law enforcement officers that ride Harley-Davidsons. This event has a poker ride, numerous vendor booths providing Harley paraphernalia, prizes, and music; all proceeds go to charities. The event begins on a Friday afternoon in September and ends Sunday morning and is usually attended by approximately 2,000 riders. The Black Sheep were asked by the promoters of this event to provide a Sunday morning worship service. This was done three years in a row and did not receive much support from non-Christians. It was found that Sunday morning after a long weekend of riding and partying, most people just wanted to go home as fast as possible. Having the services on Saturday night was not successful either. What was found to be the most effective was having a vendor's booth at the event and selling products and visiting with people as they roamed around the vendor's booths. Marty Edwards describes this type of event in this way:

> We have taken church services to motorcycle events where we have set up music—brought in a speaker. That has been marginally successful. So we're coming back and relearning a strategy that we've got to stop in any way, shape, or form expecting them to come to us. We have to go to them.

Marty Edwards maintains that Black Sheep need to "take Jesus to the streets" and to do this Black Sheep need to be on the street. At the national meeting (West Coast Rally) prior to the Laughlin River Run, Marty discussed what he felt was crucial to making an impact at the upcoming event. He stated that:

> The model—the New Testament model is to go to them. So, for example, the blessing of the bikes this year that we'll be doing at the Laughlin River Run, for the 80,000 people there, we thought about setting up a booth where riders could come and be a part of the blessing of the bikes. We thought, my goodness, if one percent of the peo-

ple came, which would be 800 or 900 people, and you only spent 30 seconds on each one, you would be there for two days. You do the math. And people aren't going to wait in line.

So rather than limit that, we decided we're going to literally go to every single rider that we can with our numbers and offer to them, "May we do a blessing of the bike for your bike?" And we'll stand there with a group of one, two, or three and actually go through a prayer, full liturgy with them, and pray for them and ask them what their needs are. Once again, the lesson that I'm still learning is we have to go. We have to go. We have to go. We can't create events where they come to us.

This event has been rather successful. Surprisingly, people were accepting of the blessing of the bikes. However, many did not seem to want to be involved with the event but were willing to let the Black Sheep bless their bikes. It seems the people who were not practicing Christians were uncomfortable with the event and others just want it done and over with.

The Laughlin River Run

The Laughlin River Run is a biker event that is held each year in Laughlin, Nevada. This event is very large with approximately 80,000 riders. It offers the same things as the other biker events but on a much larger scale. Approximately twenty five Black Sheep members went to the Laughlin River Run in 2003 and stayed for four days. The blessing of the bikes ministry took place on Thursday, Friday, and Saturday from 3:30 p.m. to 5:30 p.m. Groups of two or more Black Sheep members took their "mobile blessing of the bikes" to the streets of Laughlin, Nevada. Given that there were many different groups that were actively involved with the "mobile blessing of the bikes" the exact numbers regarding how many people were approached and offered a bike blessing and how many accepted has been estimated. Approximately seventy-five of the two hundred people that were asked if they wanted their bikes blessed agreed and many of those asked for prayer. Many of the groups that went on the "mobile blessing of the bikes" maintained that most people were open to having their bikes blessed. However, not all of the people wanted to be active in the process.

Other Events

Some of the BSHDFC chapters have a Good Friday/Black Friday ride on the Friday before Easter Sunday. They ride in staggered formation, at a very slow pace through whatever city their chapter is located. Each bike has a large black flag (approximately 3' x 5') flying behind its seat. The flag represents the crucifixion of Jesus Christ. The Black Sheep want to send a visual message about the meaning of Good Friday within the Christian religion. This ride is a solemn event to recognize the sacrifice of Jesus. However, many of the on-lookers the group rides past just stare unsure what is happening.

The events and mission work of the Black Sheep HDFC Motorcycle Ministry are ways in which the members can grow together as a group and "bring Jesus to the streets." Some members are more active than others and the reasons for this vary. Some members are only interested in attending the motorcycle events for fun and to be around other Christian riders and are not interested in the mission aspect of the group. Others are not active because they are too busy. Whatever the reasons there seems to be a core group of people who are involved in the ministry and go to most of the functions.

How active a member is in the ministry should be reflective of his or her ability to perform the role of a Black Sheep member. However, the ability to perform the role is not completely tied to how active the member is in the ministry but could be an indication of his or her desire to be seen as a biker. I noticed that most of the Black Sheep members that are active in the mission work are very committed to the ministry thus committed to the Black Sheep identity. Others who are not as active in the mission work of the Black Sheep but more active in the social aspect enjoy the membership in the Black Sheep but are not as tied to the ministry identity. In other words, it appears that some people are members to support the ministry of the Black Sheep while others are merely interested in the social aspect of the group. The extent of their commitment to the Black Sheep identity is just on different levels. Therefore it cannot be assumed that the more active the member is in the ministry the more salient his or her Black Sheep member identity because individuals may have different reasons for committing to an identity and his or her Black Sheep Member identity could be just as salient any other member.

Notes

1. http://www.christianlink.com/clubs/cma/.
2. http://www.blacksheepHDFC.org/.
3. http://www.blacksheepHDFC.org/.
4. http://www.blacksheepHDFC.org/.
5. http://www.blacksheepHDFC.org/.
6. http://www.blacksheepHDFC.org/.
7. http://www.blacksheepHDFC.org/.
8. http://www.blacksheepHDFC.org/.
9. http://www.loveride.com/.
10. Love Ride Press Release, (http://www.loveride.com/).

CHAPTER FIVE

Members of Black Sheep

This chapter examines the respondents' demographic information, childhood descriptions, motorcycle experience, and Christian background and attitudes about Christianity. The purpose of this chapter is to provide a rather in-depth introduction to the interview respondents. This chapter explores the consistencies and inconsistencies from one member to the next to determine if, in fact, patterns develop in who the members of Black Sheep HDFC are and how they came to be Christian motorcycle riders.

Demographics

Of the fifteen members interviewed there were eleven males and four females. The mean age of the subjects was forty-six years old with a range of forty to sixty-two years of age. This is consistent with mean age of the general population of Harley Riders. There were ten people who identified themselves as white/Caucasian, three people identified as Mexican, one1 person identified as Black American, and one person identified as American Indian. Twelve of the fifteen maintained that they were Republicans, one a Democrat, one Independent, and one subject had no party affiliation. Not surprisingly twelve subjects defined themselves as politically conservative, two liberal, and one claimed his political association depended on the issue. In regard to religious affiliation eleven defined themselves as Christians, two as Protestants and one as a Catholic. The type of jobs these respondents held included architect, lawyer, security manager, law enforcement, neo-natal ICU nurse, mechanic, buyer, disabled, retired, massage therapist, home appraiser, general contractor, trucker, and electrician. Twelve of the respondents considered themselves middle-class and the other three perceived themselves as upper-middle class. All respondents owned Harley-Davidson motorcycles and were members of Black Sheep HDFC Motorcycle Ministry. Length of time as members in Black Sheep HDFC varied with three of the respondents being founding members/officers, six with less than one year as members, and the rest (seven) falling somewhere between one and three years as members. Additionally, Marty Edwards, the National President and founder, was interviewed on numerous occasions.

Childhood Experiences

The questionnaire explored the childhood experiences of the respondents, asking questions about how the respondents perceived their childhoods. The point to these questions was to determine if there were any consistencies between and among respondents. Actually two patterns were found; the first pattern was many of the respondents came from families where there was divorce, and secondly, many respondents maintained they had frustrating childhood experiences.

The first notable pattern was that divorce appeared to be common among the parents of the respondents. Out of the fifteen respondents nine (sixty percent) of the parents divorced when the respondents were children and only six (forty percent) of the respondents parents stayed married throughout the respondents' childhoods. While divorce is by no means unique in today's society it was not as common in the 1960s when these respondents were children (average age of respondents was forty-six and most claimed the divorce in their family occurred when they were young). The divorce rate in 1960, around the time when the parents of these respondents were divorcing, was 2.2 divorces per 1000 population compared to 4.1 divorces per 1000 population in 2000 (U.S. Bureau of the Census, 2000). Comparatively the only time the divorce rate was lower than in 1960 was prior to World War II. In light of these statistics, the percentage of divorced parents among these respondents is rather high. The following are the responses to the questions regarding childhood descriptions and perceptions. One respondent Wayne, a security manager, described his childhood as:

> My parents were divorced when I was two. Later my mother remarried. My stepfather was in the military. Then there was a second divorce just at the time when we were all (my brothers) going into the latter part of grade school and junior high school.

Barbara, who is disabled, stated that her parents:

> divorced when I was seven years old. My family wasn't Christian at that point. After my parents got divorced, my dad started attending church but I think it was more so he could meet women.

Kate, a mechanic, claimed that her:

> parents divorced when I was very young. My mom remarried. I was raised by a stepfather who was kind of abusive towards me and he beat my mom. But we didn't know that he beat her. She ran into

doors and things like that is what she said. We did know it, but we all pretended we didn't.

Doug, a criminal defense lawyer and at this time the only Black member of Black Sheep HDFC, claimed he was:

> reared in San Francisco, California, with two brothers raised by my mom. Mom and dad divorced, I imagine when I was around three. I don't recall him ever being in the home. I began working at the age of eleven. Money was always an issue.

Similarly Ernie's childhood was also trying.

> My dad left my mom when I was three. She got married to my step-dad when I was eight or nine. He was an alcoholic. He owned an oil company. We were not poor, but my childhood—it sucked.

Another woman, Elizabeth, describes her childhood as follows:

> My childhood I would say was not excellent at all. I had a half sister, but I was not allowed to associate with her even though we lived in the same house. So my childhood [pause] I blocked out a lot. I was molested and that person died and so pretty much my prayers were answered as I thought of it. I don't know. It wasn't good. I didn't have a good childhood. We didn't have much. I never expected anything.

Elizabeth provided this information calmly and matter-of-fact as if it was just a common experience. Bill's parents were also divorced but his childhood was more self-directed. Bill is a buyer, an entrepreneur, and inventor.

> I was brought to Los Angeles area as a young child. I have one blood brother and I've never known my dad. I was raised by my grandfather. My mother lived in the house. But she was never around. I raised myself. I seriously mean that from the time I was at least four years old. I went to church by myself on my bicycle from at least six years old. I walked to school by myself. I took care of all of my needs. I did my own laundry. I had a younger brother. We took care of ourselves. I took care of him a lot, though. I was like the head of the house. I was the mom and the dad. My grandfather was around, but he had his own thing and he worked. But he was around more than my mom. I did all the stuff that a parent normally would.

Bill, however, appeared rather frustrated as he explained his childhood. He later told me that he believed his childhood was very difficult and felt anger toward all that he was required to do at such an early age. He also proudly informed me that he had custody of his only child. He apparently has taken the role of fatherhood quite seriously and seemed as if he wanted to protect his daughter from the difficulties he had to endure.

The parents of Amy, a Neo-Natal ICU Nurse, were not divorced but her family life was troubled. She describes her upbringing in the following way.

> Mom and Dad were pillars in the church. Dad led the choir and taught us singing and all that, what is referred to as worship today. It was kind of different then. Mom played the piano. What showed in public and what went on at home were extremely different. My father was very abusive; mentally and sexually. My father is now dead and I threw the first shovel of dirt on his grave.

Amy, the more vocal of the women, cried as she described her childhood. She maintained that she could see the long-term ramifications of her difficult childhood. It is interesting that all the women in this sample had rather traumatic childhoods, but none of them were necessarily angry or in denial about their childhood experiences.

However, not all members' parents were divorced or recalled their family life as difficult. David, an architect, felt his childhood was good. He described his family life as follows:

> My father was an optometrist. My mother was a dental hygienist. They raised five of us kids in Detroit. We were middle class, maybe upper middle class. We had a good family. Good up-bringing.

Later, David did inform me that his father was an alcoholic and claimed that at times that was problematic, but overall he maintained that his childhood was good. Roger, who is in law enforcement, remembers his childhood as good also.

> My father worked forty-four years as a warehouse man for Thrifty drug. He supplemented that income with a part-time job of about thirty-eight years at Sears and Roebuck working the receiving dock. My mother also worked for over twenty years for General Motors in the warehouse for them. So they had three incomes to support their four children. They did that to be able to provide for us. We all went to Catholic school. I went to Catholic school from kindergarten through the ninth grade. I had a very good childhood.

The high rate of divorce and the apparent dissatisfaction with childhood appear to be consistent patterns among the interviewees. Of course this does not provide the answers as to why the respondents became Christian bikers but it does lay the groundwork for finding similarities among the members of Black Sheep HDFC.

Motorcycle Experience and Background

Another area that the interview schedule addressed was past experience with motorcycles. The reason for asking questions regarding motorcycle experience is to determine if riding a motorcycle is a fairly new phenomenon for many of the respondents or part of a life-long relationship with motorcycles. Most of the respondents rode dirt bikes as young adults and then after marriage could not afford motorcycles, so the motorcycle and the lifestyle was terminated until their children were raised and had moved out of the house. So, they did not identify as a biker for a better part of their life. Most of these respondents were new to riding a Harley and the Harley-Davidson subculture. In response to the questions regarding motorcycle history or past experience the respondents answered in the following ways. Wayne claims:

> Oh, I was probably in my twenties. Actually my brothers took me out and taught me how to ride. Not until 1999 was my first time I had a Harley. I had a different one than I have now. I used to ride on the back of friends' motorcycles in high school but that was a long time ago when there were no helmet laws. Most of the twenty years that my wife and I were married we really didn't have the finances to go out and buy a motorcycle. So when we finally did back in 1999. This is when we really became active.

David maintained that he was involved with off road motorcycles at young age but did not get into street type bikes until he was in his late fifties.

> I started riding dirt bikes in like 1961. Ran with a group of people down in the Costa Mesa area, my neighbors, introduced me to motorcycling: dirt biking. I probably rode two and a half maybe three years with them. And then quit racing in the dirt and did not ride motorcycles for probably almost thirty-five years. Then in 1999, we bought our Harley, and been riding that almost four years.

Nathan's family was opposed to the Harley-Davidson motorcycle groups of the late 1960s and 1970s, so he owned many different types of motorcycles.

> I had mini-bikes when I was eleven and twelve years old. And I worked on my uncle's motorcycles. They (my uncles) were in outlaw bike clubs, so I grew up around all that. My family didn't want me to have that lifestyle. So owning a Harley was, at times, a problem but I have owned everything from rice rockets to Harley-Davidsons.

Elizabeth, one of the female members of Black Sheep HDFC described her past motorcycle experience in this way.

> I made myself start riding at about the age of fifteen. I was not brought up in any type of environment like that, but my first boyfriend liked to ride a dirt bike. So, he taught me to ride. I rode dirt bikes until about '92. I was about thirty when I got into street bikes Hondas and all that stuff. Then my step-dad willed me his Triumph and later in 2002, I bought my Harley.

Chris is an example of how the responsibilities of parenthood cramp the motorcyclist's lifestyle.

> I used to race dirt bikes. When I was eighteen, I bought a friend's Yamaha street bike. I rode that for six months and bought a Harley. I rode that up until '79 right before I got married. I sold it. Then had children, raised them and then bought a new Harley in 2000. I've been riding ever since.

Another example of giving up riding while raising children is Roger's story.

> My first experience with motorcycles was riding friends' motorcycles as a young teenager. I rode dirt bikes. I used to have a circle of friends at the time that used to go—not the motor cross—but the desert racing. I would go to desert races and I would ride when my friends were generous enough to share their dirt bikes with me. When I was twenty-one years old, right after getting discharged from the Marine Corps, I bought my first Harley-Davidson. It was a brand new 1970 Sportster. I had that Sportster for a short period of time. After I got married, we sold the bike for a down payment on the first house. My next bike was in 2001 another Harley-Davidson.

Amy, another female member of Black Sheep, felt the effects of being a female in a male world.

> My mother told me only bad girls ride bikes, because I used to look out the window and see bikes go by and I was so intrigued by them. And when my brothers got into dirt bikes, I stood in the grass in the front yard just because they told me I shouldn't like bikes. I always loved them but they always said only bad people get involved with bikes. So, you know I just started riding. We would take turns on the dirt bikes. It was just something we did up and down the street until the things fell apart and dad wouldn't fix them. I bought myself a Sportster and started riding with the Black Sheep a little over a year ago.

Not all respondents have histories of riding motorcycles. Kate is new to the world of riding, although, she looks more like a biker than most of the members of Black Sheep HDFC. She has many tattoos and has been known to wear her hair in an orange mohawk. She rides on the back of the bike behind her husband.

> Just a year ago we got the Road King. I have never been part of that at all—that biker stuff, but it was just funny that we got the bike and it's like I'd always been a biker. I always had that kind of an attitude that whole set apart thing.

Marty Edwards didn't just want to ride a motorcycle he wanted to ride a Harley. This is the kind of attitude and buyer loyalty Harley-Davidson Corporation worked so hard to develop. In Marty's case it was successful.

> I didn't start riding until 1998. I've never really owned a motorcycle. I think I had a moped or something when I was younger, but never really owned a motorcycle until 1998. I started looking at motorcycles, I wasn't sure I was going to be able to afford a Harley-Davidson. My wife said, "Why don't you buy this one? It's so much less." And I said, "I don't mean to be a spoiled brat, but, quite honestly, if I can't have a Harley, I would just as soon not ride." And I meant that. That's not a sense of loyalty; that's just the way I felt.

Apparently for these respondents riding motorcycles as a young person has had some affect on motorcycle ownership as an adult. However, it seems that the ownership and identity as a Harley rider is more important than the riding itself. Interestingly, most of the respondents did not ride Harleys until they were adults. They were more involved with off road bikes as young people. It is not surprising that the respondents would prefer street bikes, even touring bikes because off road riding is more appropriate for the young. However, choosing to ride a Harley-Davidson over other makes and models is interesting. This could be due to the romanticized image of the Harley rider now portrayed by the Harley-Davidson Corporation or that owning a Harley-Davidson can be viewed as a status symbol. Many members purchased their Harleys in the late 1990s and early 2000 right around the time the Black Sheep ministry began.

Christianity

The next area the interview schedule examined was when and how the respondents became Christians and how the respondents define themselves as Christians. The reasons for these questions were to determine the extent the respondents identify with Christianity. The interview schedule specifically examined the length of time each respondent had been a Christian, how they became Christians, if their co-workers, neighbors, and friends knew they were Christians (to determine if they were openly Christian), and how committed they are to Christianity. Most respondents have defined themselves as Christians for many years. However, there are a few respondents that were either new Christians, or have returned to Christianity when they became involved with Black Sheep HDFC. A frequent response to how the respondents defined themselves as Christians had to do with their belief in Jesus Christ and their Salvation.

Becoming a Christian

Wayne has not always considered himself a Christian. Wayne used to be in law enforcement and he still carries himself like a cop. He was often reluctant to provide personal information. I was not surprised to find out that he had been in law enforcement and now in corporate security. He has a very watchful demeanor. He states that:

> I think when I actually came back to Christianity was when I came into Black Sheep in 2002. I have been a practicing Christian at different times in my life. Well, you know, my mother being Italian, she was really strong Catholic. So she was always pushing the religion and I would go to church. I sort of left the church, I think, probably when my brother died. I had a real struggle with that. He died in a car accident. I had a real hard time with that. I kind of moved away from Christ. When I went into police work I started to come back to Christ because I realized that I couldn't do that job without having Christ in my life. When I got out of police work it's like I lost Christ again. I think it's because of the nature of the work I did before. I mean—I'm serious. There was not a night or a call that I went on that I didn't pray that Christ was with me. I needed his help because it was pretty frightening and difficult time.

Barbara describes her Christian life in this way.

> I was sitting there in church and I felt the call of the Lord in my life. It was a combination of things. I was one of these people that never felt like I belonged anywhere. Not so much within my family but I always felt out of place like there was something different about me. I accepted Christ at church when I was thirteen. I was into church up until the time I was about seventeen years old, and then I got busy in high school sports. I kind of fell away from the church for a while. Then I met Ernie, my husband, and he wasn't a Christian and he dragged me further away from the Lord than I was. We just had a really rough time being married and I decided at some point I had to turn back to the Lord.

Barbara defines herself as a "weak" Christian. Kate defines her Christianity as "having a personal relationship with Jesus" yet her story is difficult.

> I became a Christian when I was fifteen. When I was in high school, someone invited me to a Campus Life—Youth for Christ meeting. One of the counselors gave me a ride home. I accepted Christ in the car out in front of my house. Then when I went in the house my mom just beat the crap out of me because she said I was in the car kissing some boy and she was embarrassed and mad. She really beat me bad. I wasn't allowed to go to church. My mom didn't allow that at all.

Bill was raised Catholic and was very attached to the symbolic and ritual elements of Christianity.

> I went to catechism and did my confirmation all at an early, young age. I always believed in God. I can explain that by the fact that I wore a Scapula. It's a little cloth thing that has a picture of Mary on it. The front looks the same as the back. It was believed that if you are wearing the Scapula when you die then Mary will intercede and speak to the Father. I wore that all the time. It was just an outward sign of my commitment to Jesus Christ. I forgot it at somebody's house one day and I had to go back and get it. When I went back to get it, they asked me what it was. I said oh, nothing and I left. Then I got about a block away and I realized that I had denied Jesus Christ because I had said "oh, nothing." So I went back to the house and I explained to them what the Scapula was to me. They just looked like, why did you have to tell us this. But I had known that I had denied my Lord. This happened when I was in the seventh grade.

Nathan claims he became a Christian when he was twelve years old "during the Jesus Freak Movement in 1972 at Morgan Park in Covina, California. It was when I heard the bells ringing." He defines Christianity as "personal, I hold Christ very strongly in my life. It's not often that I share how I feel with other people because that's just who I am. It is just the kind of person I am. But it's a very, very big part of my life." Nathan is ex-military and ex-law enforcement. Similar to Wayne he also carries himself like a cop, he is private and watchful. Nathan at times can seem very unapproachable.

Amy defines her Christianity as "unorthodox." She has had a rather rocky road to Christianity. She describes the last twenty-five years this way:

> I grew up in the church because I grew up that way it was never really of that much value or special to me. I didn't realize how important it was until later when I totally screwed up so bad. This was in 1982. I was on drugs—big time. And I had to get out. I had hit rock bottom. I had found Christ but things were tough for many years and then in the late 1990s my son told me about a church. He said "I went to this place a couple of times and they're all a bunch of broken people. They're all either divorced or ex-drug addicts. He told me you'll fit right in, mom." So I went, and I do.

Amy told me that:

> My friends know I am a Christian. They know I love God with all my heart. But I can't be stuffy. I have a mouth on me sometimes. I don't try and hide my imperfections from my friends and co-workers. I've never had one of them ask me how I can be a Christian and talk like that or how I can be a Christian and do that. They know me in spite of me. They know I love God. They know I ride a bike. They know I ride a bike for Jesus. They know I belong to a Christian motorcycle club. But they think I'm crazy.

Marty, the president of Black Sheep HDFC, claims:

> I became a Christian when I was much younger. I don't remember
> how old I was, probably five or six years old. And then I got very se-
> rious about following Christ when I was fourteen. From that point
> forward, I began to understand and be able to articulate my faith. As
> with most people between ages of five and fourteen, a lot of things
> come—adolescence and all of that—and so I had to re-understand
> what it meant to be a Christian when I was fourteen. I was at a spe-
> cial revival service for teenagers and gave my life to Christ. That's
> the time I remember and can say, yes, from that moment forward, I
> made a concerted effort to follow Christ.

Marty defines his Christian walk as:

> I not only believe but live in my understanding of the claims and
> standards of Christ. It's not just a mental assent, if that's the right
> word; it is a submission to, a radical submission to the claim of the
> Bible, the sixty-six books in the Bible. I don't know of anybody who
> knows me who doesn't know exactly how I feel about Christ.

Ernie found Christ in a unique fashion during the summer of 1986.

> I went to Knott's Berry Farm. I was talking with Larry Norman who
> is a Christian musician. He asked me if I wanted to accept the Lord
> and we prayed underneath Montezuma's revenge. I have been a
> Christian since then. I guess I am just average Christian. I don't
> know everything. I don't try to pretend I know everything. There's
> lots of stuff that makes no sense to me. But it's in the Bible so I be-
> lieve it.

John's acceptance of Christianity came as a surprise to him.

> I became a Christian at nineteen. I was working for the family busi-
> ness at the time and my friend became Christian and was constantly
> telling my friend Steve and I about how he was saved. We continued
> to threaten to beat him up about it if he wouldn't shut up. He was a
> little over-exuberant. He saw us as going to go to hell. You know
> the standard things that repel non-Christians. He challenged me to
> just once go to his church and if I did he would never mention it
> again. So at nineteen years old, I thought that was a good deal. I de-
> cided I would go one time for an hour and never have to listen to an-
> yone again. So I went and really enjoyed it. After about three months
> I felt like, you know, this is truth. It was an intellectual decision
> there was no emotion involved in it at all. It was presented to me, I
> believed it, and so I committed my life because I believed it. But, you
> know, if you ask me if I back slide from time to time, well, of course.

Chris, the massage therapist, defines a Christian as follows:

> To me being a Christian means when there's a time in your life when you become born again when you ask Jesus to be your Savior and realizing that you're now a child of God you have to obey him. We get our instructions from the Bible. So you have to be in the Bible to understand what he wants us to do. Then it's a struggle, you know, to follow that. It's never easy. Because, you know we are who we are from the life we lived before. But I've learned anyway through faith that you just trust God even when you don't do the right thing. You just ask for forgiveness and start over again. You know, I expect him to help me get over whatever it was and get through and get on track again.

David has been a practicing Christian for many years.

> I became a Christian in 1972 through Calvary Chapel Costa Mesa. I have walked with the Lord ever since. I came through a lot of crap through my teenage years and through my early twenties. I have often wondered how and why I made it that far without being killed or in prison for the rest of my life. I am just a believer in the Lord Jesus Christ accepting him as my Lord and my Savior and letting him live through me.

All the respondents identified as Christian although their definition of Christianity or being a Christian differed. Seemingly, Black Sheep Harley-Davidsons for Christ Motorcycle Ministry is a place for people to be "Christian" but to a certain degree to be a "Christian" in their own way. Many of the respondents came from difficult childhood backgrounds and were looking for a place to belong when they joined the Black Sheep. They found membership in the Black Sheep a place to be unique.

Asking the respondents how they became Christians and how they define themselves as Christians was interesting and seemingly, at least to the respondents, the questions were reasonable. However, asking questions regarding how the respondents learned to be a Christian brought forth a variety of replies. Every respondent told me the question "How did you learn to be a Christian" was a good question, but they were rather confused as to how to answer. I found their interest and confusion in the questions as remarkable as the answers they gave to the question. Learning the role of Christianity or how to be a Christian for these respondents differed. How to portray the role of the Christian lacked consensus among the respondents as well. The interviewees disagreed as to what determines a "successful" Christian and they also disagreed as to how easy or difficult the role of Christian is to play or portray. How they felt other members portrayed Christianity was problematic as well. All respondents appeared to have a basic idea as to what a Christian identity or role should be.

Learning How to Be a Christian

This is how Nathan described how he learned to be a Christian.

> My main education, what I believe Christianity is, is self-study from
> the Bible. Watching other people that I thought were good examples
> of what, in my mind, a Christian should be and trying to imitate or to
> be more like them.

Kate claims she was born a Christian. "I was born that way when I was fifteen (born again). I didn't learn to be a Christian. I was born again." Bill
learned how to be a Christian by "reading the Bible and knowing more and more
by reading about Christianity and trying to follow His example." Chris' understanding of how one learns to be a Christian is more complex.

> Learning to be a Christian, I think is different than learning to be
> something else in life. Because the things we learn in life, we learn
> from our parents. We learn from things that are going on around us.
> But to be a Christian, not only is that happening, but you also have to
> study God's word. And if you don't study God's word, you're not
> going to understand what it is to be a Christian, you can act like a
> Christian, but what happens when you're alone and nobody is around.
> The only way you learn what sin is, what's right and what's wrong, is
> through God's word.

John states:

> I don't think I learned how to be a Christian. As soon as I accepted
> Christ, I think obviously, that's what made me a Christian. But how
> did I learn that? How did I formulate my belief system within that
> Christianity? A lot of study. You know, I've never been a pew-
> sitter. That's never been the place I would get my information. I've
> got a wall loaded with books about Christianity. Half of them worth-
> less, half of them are great.

Marty described the process of learning to be a Christian in this way.

> Well, that's a tough one. I guess just a personal relationship with Je-
> sus Christ. I don't really recall a lot of pastors back in the '70s really
> telling you how to live a Christian life. I know for darn sure that
> none of the pastors that I sat under ever taught me how to share the
> Lord with other people and bring them to Christ. It wasn't until
> probably within the last ten years that I have actually learned that.
> Even though I was planting seeds in my youth, I didn't realize that
> was what I was doing. I do know that the role of a Christian comes
> with a great deal of responsibility, and nothing with that much re-
> sponsibility is easy.

Amy's response to the question regarding how one learns to be a Christian was "I don't know that I'm there yet." Another respondent told me learning to be a Christian was "an ongoing process." Another posited that:

> you should continually follow the example of Christ in the Scriptures. The Spirit of the God has been promised to teach us the truth in all things. Unfortunately, people also learn by looking at others. And that is Scriptural too because Paul said, "Follow me as I follow Christ." But it's scary because there are some poor examples of Christians and many end up following a poor example and in turn they end up being a poor example of what a Christian themselves.

How one learns to be a Christian differs, at least to some degree, for most of the respondents. Similarly, the role or persona is apparently not easy to portray for most of the respondents. Many find themselves trying to live up to some sort of standard while others feel the role of Christian is to be played out through letting the Holy Spirit live in them, thus letting Christ perform the role. There is certainly diversity in the answers given by the respondents. While how one learns to be a Christian differed among respondents, all respondents seemed clear on what was the "right" behavior for Christians. However, they did not actually believe "right behavior" could be achieved easily.

The Role of the Christian

Wayne describes the role of a Christian as:

> It's very difficult. I mean it's easy to be bad and hard to be good because you're surrounded by society which is not always the best role model for anybody. So it's very easy to be bad in society and it's difficult to be good.

John agrees with Wayne in regard to the pressures of society affecting the role of Christian. He states that:

> the role of Christian is not easy to portray because there are so many stereotypes and so many preconceived ideas of what a Christian is. And it's the fault of Christians that it is that way. Because there are so many different people who call themselves Christians and they all have a different way of thinking. Just as a simple example: Dancing. You have one group that says "no dancing" and one group that says "dancing is okay." And it scatters from there. I hate telling people I'm a Christian right off. Then they lay their preconceived ideas on me. That's one of the reasons I don't tell them. I don't want to say I'm Christian. Because their last experience with a Christian may have been "you're a sinner and you're going to hell." Now all of a sudden I'm one of those people. I think it's very difficult.

Conversely, others maintain that the role of Christian is an easy role. Kate maintains that the role of Christian is easy claiming "God the father, Holy Spirit, is in me to where I can't even help but be a Christian and not just act like a Christian." Doug maintains that the role really has nothing to do with him. All he has to do is accept Jesus Christ as his Savior. "A lot of folks don't understand the gift of salvation. It's not something you work for. All acts are dirty rags before Christ. The hardest part is accepting the gift and it's a daily walk."

There seem to be two thoughts in relation to the level difficulty in performing the role of a Christian. One line of thought suggests that to play the role of a Christian it is necessary to conscientiously consider your actions and thoughts. In short, that the role of Christian takes agency. On the other hand, there are others that believe that to play the role of Christian is to let Christ, the Holy Spirit, live through them and that human agency does not play a part in performing the role of Christian. This, of course, plays havoc with identity theory because it maintains that identity and role behavior is out of the hands of the individual.

Others seemed concerned with the inconsistencies between one Christian and another in regard to being "good" Christians. The diversity of expected or acceptable Christian attitudes and behaviors creates for some respondents a fear of hypocrisy.

Conclusion

This chapter is full of rich data that was derived from the in-depth interviews with the fifteen respondents. Consistent with Harley-Davidson demographic information, the median age of the respondents in this study is forty-seven. In addition, the income level is also similar to the information gathered by Harley-Davidson Corporation. The demographical data derived from the interviews is valuable because it supports previous research and provides a framework for additional data.

Two patterns or themes were found when examining childhood experiences. The first was a high rate of divorce among the families of the respondents. Although divorce is common today it was not common in the 1960s when these respondents were children. The second theme was that many of the respondents claimed to have come from difficult or dysfunctional families. This is not uncommon either but it is a consistency that was found among the respondents.

Many of respondents rode dirt bikes as children or young adults but did not have street bikes until recently. Most of the respondents discussed owning dirt bikes when young and some even had street bikes in their early twenties. However, none of the respondents in this study claimed to have owned bikes of any sort while raising their children. It was after the children were raised that many of the respondents bought their motorcycles. The purchase of a Harley-Davidson motorcycle was a new prospect for all but one of the respondents. In fact, a couple of the respondents bought a Harley-Davidson primarily for the purpose of riding with the Black Sheep HDFC, but claimed they wanted to own a Harley as well. These reasons support my earlier statements regarding the effects of creative marketing techniques and media influence on Harley sales. The Harley-Davidson Corporation demographical information claims that fifty-seven percent of all Harley buyers are first time Harley owners.[1] It also supports my statements regarding the desire to have a persona (identity) that they feel is exciting and can be easily purchased through the ownership of a Harley-Davidson.

Most of the respondents have been Christians for many years. Many accepted Christ when young or in their teens. One member became a Christian at a Christian concert, another in a theme park, and another late at night alone in his bedroom. Other roads to Christianity have been more tragic and rocky. The respondents found the question regarding how they learned to be a Christian interesting but had differing ideas as to how Christianity is learned. Some believed you learned through reading the Bible, others through watching other Christians, and some believed you do not learn to be a Christian you become a Christian through the Holy Spirit. The ease or difficulty of playing the role of a Christian differed in the same way. Some believed playing the role of a Christian is difficult and a huge responsibility and others believe it is not difficult because it is the work of the Holy Spirit.

In regard to identity it seems that these respondents feel they need to increase their network of Christians to become "better Christians." This increases their ability to perform the role and, therefore, commit to the identity. Consequently, the more time they spend with other Christians the more comfortable they are with their own performance, or ability to be a "Christian." In fact, it seems that these respondents were more cognizant of what is a "bad" Christian than what is a "good" Christian. This must create some problem with exacting the right role behavior for the role of Christian and in the case of a Christian biker the correct behavior would seemingly be even more unclear.

Notes

1. http://investor.Harley-Davidson.com/demographics.cfm?locale=en_US&bmLocale=en_US

CHAPTER SIX

Becoming a Member of Black Sheep

This final data focuses on the identity of a Christian biker and the Black Sheep member and how these identities are maintained, manipulated, and perpetuated over time and space. In addition, this final data examines which identity, Christian or biker, is more salient to each respondent. Essentially Chapter four provided a rather in-depth exploration of what is the Black Sheep Harley-Davidsons for Christ Motorcycle Ministry, how it began, and its mission. Chapter five presented the demographic data, information of childhood experiences, motorcycle background and experience and the descriptions of how each respondent interviewed became Christians. This chapter brings together all of the earlier data with this final data to create a comprehensive view of the Black Sheep HDFC Motorcycle Ministry and its members.

This last data chapter examines what it means to be a Black Sheep member and covers numerous aspects of the membership including how and why the respondents became part of the Black Sheep Harley-Davidsons for Christ Motorcycle Ministry. Secondly, this chapter looks at how the respondents learned to be bikers (role expectations). The third area focuses on both the biker and Christian biker image. Lastly, the chapter explores the respondent's understanding of the Black Sheep HDFC ministry and its mission.

Important to understanding how the respondents have developed their Christian biker identity is to inquire into how and why they became members of Black Sheep HDFC and to question their understandings of the ministry's core beliefs. Of interest is determining if all respondents understand the mission of Black Sheep HDFC in the same way and in which ways are they actively involved with the ministry. Furthermore exploring the positive and negative feelings the respondents may have toward the group will also be of importance to determine not only how they relate to the group but also their willingness to be defined as part of the group, their interactional and affective commitment. This next section will detail the events that prompted the respondents to become members of Black Sheep HDFC.

Becoming a Member of Black Sheep HDFC

Wayne explains his membership in Black Sheep in this way:

> I went to a couple of rallies and I kept seeing the Black Sheep and I would just watch in the background because I wasn't too sure what they were really about, were they sincere, the whole thing. At that point in my life, I was really going to the extreme. I had the vest with all the crude sayings and all those things. I don't even know why I did that. Then one day a guy came up to me and invited me to a Black Sheep meeting.

Wayne's attraction to Black Sheep is more complex than most of the other respondents. He responded to this question in this way:

> Because of the work I've done, I really haven't had a lot of friends. Being a police officer, you have police officer friends. Cops aren't always the most amiable people to be around. So I didn't have a lot of police friends. The ones I did have, unfortunately, I fell into the same habits they had—drinking after work. It wasn't a great environment. So when I left that arena, you know with cops you're either in or you are out. And I was out. So hmmm. I had no friends. Then I got into the corporate environment and because of the position there I found it was very difficult to have friends. So, I just realized, you know, that, hey, here you are in your fifties and you don't have a friend in the world. I wanted to have friendships, but I wanted them to be Christian friends because I was tired of, you know, I was playing a role or being somebody else all the time and I just wanted to be myself and be accepted for me.

Wayne has both positive and negative feelings about Black Sheep HDFC and notes the lack of participation by all members.

> Well, you know, the whole concept, everything around the group is positive, what they represent, what they want to do. The negative part is that I don't get the sense that there's a hundred percent buy in or participation. There are times, I know, when there have been gatherings the Black Sheep participation was pretty sparse.

Similar to Wayne, who also was also in law enforcement, Roger did not join Black Sheep right away. He was more cautious than most members.

> Initially I became aware of Black Sheep through a Christian friend of mine. I was skeptical of Black Sheep because of being a gang cop for

fourteen years, and having personal friends that are motorcycle gang detectives. I don't have any expertise in motorcycle gangs, the outlaw gangs, but I just felt this patch thing and the membership—I just wasn't interested. But then I met the founder of Black Sheep HDFC, Marty Edwards, and several pastors. Actually, one of them which is my pastor. And my defensive guard went down and my stereotyping of them changed tremendously.

Barbara and her husband Ernie became members because they went to Lamb's Fellowship church and Marty Edwards invited them to become involved with the Black Sheep HDFC. What attracted Barbara to Black Sheep HDFC was the:

fact that it was an avenue for Christians to be able to ride and fellowship with people. Ernie and me we're just different. We don't fit into the normal Christian environment. I don't wear pearls around my neck I don't like singing hymns out of books. I thought this group was a good fit for us.

Barbara is an active member and has mostly negative feelings toward the group.

Well [pause] I wished they rode faster. It just seems like we have a geriatric crowd that seems to be leading the way. Also, I'm not really happy with some of the decisions that are made. I think that too few people are making the decisions for a large group. I don't want to say anything negative, because I understand the purpose of Black Sheep. But right now I'm not getting as much out of Black Sheep as I had hoped.

David also became part of Black Sheep HDFC through attending Lamb's Fellowship.

David, currently the president of one Southern California Chapter of Black Sheep, maintains that Black Sheep HDFC is a

wonderful outreach to the unsaved motorcycling world. But the thing I don't care for about Black Sheep is most of the members of Black Sheep do not have the heart of the evangelist and outreach. This is what Black Sheep is all about. Many members are involved for the fun rides and the fellowship. The whole purpose of Black Sheep is to go out and reach people that don't know Christ that ride motorcycles. This is where we need to grow. The mission of Black Sheep is to reach out to the motorcycling world and to bring the good news to them.

Elizabeth, who had been around bikes most of her life, was looking for a place to belong when she found Black Sheep.

It had to have been a God thing because I was really lost. I didn't have a bike. I wanted to hang around bikers—that is what I've always been into. I wrote to Marty Edwards to be on the Black Sheep mailing list. The only reason I bought the Harley is because if I wanted to

be involved with Black Sheep, I had to have a Harley. I had vowed
never to own a Harley because I did not want the name. I didn't want
to pay for the name, because it was just the status of owning a Harley
and I've never been like that.

Elizabeth is rather amused by the whole idea of Black Sheep HDFC Motorcycle
Ministry. She claims "it's an oxymoron because it is kind of like a jumbo shrimp
type of thing, Christian bikers."

Elizabeth sees herself as an active member and has only positive feelings
toward Black Sheep. "The Black Sheep they don't care what you have done,
which is how it should be with Christians. They'll help you out if you ask for
prayer. The whole thing all pertains to Jesus."

Kate became part of Black Sheep because she had read about Black Sheep
in the *Christian Times* newspaper. Kate is really interested in evangelism and
wants to be actively involved with the ministry. She states:

> Black Sheep's ministry was to the HOG members. The people that
> think they're good people because they never killed anybody and so
> when they die they're going to be standing in the—I never killed an-
> ybody line. They won't understand how come they're going to hell. I
> have always had a heart for those people. That's the HOG people,
> they're good people just going to hell. So that's what attracted me to
> Black Sheep I have a heart for these people.

Kate is an active member of a Southern California chapter and she also holds the
position as the chapter treasurer. She has both positive and negative feelings
toward the Black Sheep HDFC Motorcycle Ministry.

> The positive feelings I have are all the great potential I see in Black
> Sheep for ministry outreach. The negative feelings are—we've had a
> lot of weirdos in our chapter. Oh, it's so bad. It's like we just attract
> the weirdest people. There are some really strange people. I don't
> know what that's all about.

Kate's husband, Bill, is the President of the same Southern California Chapter
contends that:

> the positive feelings I have about Black Sheep are that it's a great op-
> portunity to fellowship with other like-minded believers that have the
> common interest of riding motorcycles as transportation. I enjoy out-
> reach events and letting other riders know that we're not as alien as
> they might think. We are alien, but not in the ways that they think.
> We like to ride hard. We enjoy buying chrome for our bikes. We like
> to do all the same things as they do. With the exception of that we
> have a purpose driven life unlike many people in the world. My nega-
> tive feelings towards Black Sheep are probably not any different than
> any other organization, and that's any time you work with volunteers,
> they're just that. They are volunteers that do what they want and
> don't always necessarily live up to what they may have said they

would do. Christians always seem to have their pat answers that they use that they think relieves them of any obligation they may have made like church, family, or some other higher call that they feel that God has put on them that allows them to back out of any commitments that they have made.

Chris was attracted to Black Sheep because:

> Well, the fact that I like to ride and I was kind of over the outlaw biker scene from the old days. Then I realized that Black Sheep is a true ministry. It's a place where I know I can go and just show up and everybody will say "Hey how you doing? Where you've been? What's going on?" It's friendship. The only negative thing I can see that came out of it was, you know, in the beginning there was a lot of people didn't understand what it was about. They thought it was just another biker club, you know. We're a ministry, not a gang.

Amy joined Black Sheep because, like many of the others, she felt it was a group of people in which she could feel comfortable:

> I have been a "Black Sheep" all my life in my family. My brothers, they're both pastors and neither one of them have ever agreed with my liberal Christian lifestyle. My mom always thought I was a renegade. But she loves me. I've always been a Black Sheep. So it's like I don't feel like I have to fit in to fit in. I can be just me. Because they're all just them. Although just like any other group, people just talk too much. They can't keep their mouth to themselves sometimes and that's whether you're at work or at church or at school. Everybody is always talking.

Marty, the National President of Black Sheep HDFC, maintains:

> I feel very positive about the group. I'm having more fun in ministry than I've ever had before in my life. I've been in the ministry for thirty years. One person's response to that was, well, sure, if I could ride around the country on a motorcycle, I would think that would be fun too. It really has nothing to do with motorcycles. Most of my work with the Black Sheep is done behind a computer or on the phone or e-mail, when it works. I'm pulling together Christians from across the country to take that machine in the garage, to use it as a tool for ministry, which, if you go back to my history, is something I've always tried to do; that is to mobilize the church. Now I've found that there's at least one group that can be mobilized to use their motorcycles for ministry, which is good.

Marty explains his negative feelings he has with Black Sheep but he maintains it is more of a frustration than anything negative:

> I would say my biggest challenge would be even within Black Sheep there are church people there, it's to get them to break out of a church

minded mode and become street Christians. You know, world Christians. So that would be the tension. I don't mean tension [pause] stress. I mean that would be the tension between the joy and the frustration. But there is by far and away more joy in Black Sheep than tension.

Ernie saw a flier at one of the Harley-Davidson dealership advertising the Black Sheep HDFC. Ernie was attracted to Black Sheep "because of the name I figured I was a black sheep my whole life, so it seemed like people I could hang out with." Ernie is an active member and the vice president of a Southern California Chapter and has both positive feelings and negative feelings about the group. John learned about Black Sheep HDFC through a newspaper story.

> I saw that article in the newspaper about Black Sheep being in a parade and there was a phone number. So I called. I think what the ministry does is fantastic. I think outreach to HOG is really important. Although, I think the group minimizes the group's fun aspect of it too much. Marty often says, this isn't a group for people to get together to go on great rides. It's a ministry. I think it can be both and do both equally well.

In summary, Black Sheep HDFC Motorcycle Ministry offers most of its members a family or group in which to belong and people in which to identify, with many of the members stating that they have always been on the outside looking in never really fitting into the world around them. They have found in Black Sheep HDFC, a place of acceptance, friendship, and a family. Some have joined Black Sheep HDFC because they felt it was a great way to witness to non-believers. However, for some the opportunity to witness appears to be secondary.

Most members find that the positive elements of Black Sheep HDFC lie in the opportunity to spread the Gospel and to be part of a group of like-thinkers. Many maintained the benefit of being able to ride a Harley and witness at the same time as particularly advantageous. Furthermore, the opportunity to ride with clean and sober riders was another area that the respondents found favorable.

As in most groups the things that the respondents found that were negative were the lack of complete participation, and frustrating decision-making processes. Many felt that a lot of the members did not participate fully and that when they did it was, generally, in relation to having fun and riding together, not the mission work. This has left a few of the members to do the work of the rest of the group. Of course this is not uncommon problem within groups and group behavior. It seems some want to have the identity of a Christian biker, but do not really want to put in the work that supports the Black Sheep Harley-Davidsons for Christ Ministry mission statement. Seemingly, they want the outward appearance of the Christian biker but not necessarily the responsibility. Also, some felt that there should be greater democracy in relation to how decisions are made. I am not sure if this perceived lack of democracy is a function of a dictatorship or, again, just the lack of participation by some members, to be actively involved with all aspects of membership including attending meetings where decisions are made.

Mission and Expectations

The next area that the interview schedule explored was the expectations the members had about the ministry and the other members within the ministry. The reason these types of questions were asked was to determine if the image the respondent had of him or herself in regard to being a Black Sheep HDFC member agreed with the image they had of the other members. Another reason was to examine whether the respondents believed that the entire ministry had the same understandings of both the mission of Black Sheep HDFC and the image they portrayed as a group and as individuals. The questionnaire also explored the various kinds of activities that Black Sheep HDFC participate in and to what extent all members are involved with these activities. From the following answers there does not appear to be any firm consensus as to what exactly is the mission of Black Sheep HDFC. What's more, the members do not really seem to know much about the mission work and activities of the Black Sheep HDFC ministry.

Marty Edwards, the founder and national president, defines the mission of Black Sheep as:

> The mission of Black Sheep is to make Christ known to the motorcycle world and then to introduce those people to the local church. That's more ministry and more responsibility than some people want to own. So there are those who have heard that ten times and it still hasn't caught on yet. They truly don't understand the mission. They haven't grasped it or discovered it yet. Then there are those who I think understand it but this is still just "my place to come and hang out and be with friends." That's not all that different from the church or a lot of other organizations, because people are different and their needs are different. And no matter how clear a communicator you are, your words will always go through people's filters. Some see Black Sheep as a tremendous opportunity to reach out to nonbelievers for Christ. Others see it as another support group for them to receive love and care and ministry. Others see it as just a fun place to ride where people ride and don't drink. They don't want to ride with people that drink.

Marty maintains that most members participate within Black Sheep.

> Overwhelmingly, the majority of members are active. The few who don't participate are probably phasing out. Then we have other activities that are varying levels of intensity in terms of ministry. Everything from simply going down and serving the food at a HOG event to visiting injured riders in the hospital, to passing out tracts in Laughlin, to performing a blessing of the bikes for riders, to picking up broken-down motorcycles at major motorcycle events in trailers

and taking them someplace for repair. So we find any way that we can communicate love, the love of Christ, to motorcycle riders.

Clearly, not all members understood the ministry's mission the way Marty does. Wayne was asked if he felt all members had the same expectation of the Black Sheep HDFC and if they understood the mission in the same way. He explained that the mission of Black Sheep HDFC "is to make Christ known to other Harley-Davidson enthusiasts. To bring Christianity to HOG members to promote basically the idea that bikers or Harley-Davidson enthusiasts aren't a bunch of outlaws." Wayne was asked what kind of mission work and activities do the Black Sheep support. He responded with:

> Well, from what I have been involved with, there have been, for ex-ample, people that are ill or in the hospital that we go and visit. I know they've gotten together to help support folks financially, emo-tionally, or spiritually. They are always looking out for each other. At least that's my impression. I know that they are always trying to spread the Word of Christ. And that's really it. So there's a lot of involvement, I think in the community and in the membership.

David knows the mission of the Black Sheep HDFC and is able to describe the various mission and activities in which the ministry participates.

> As far as ministry, we do what Jesus said. We go. We go out into the world of the unbeliever. Not all members participate and I'm kind of sad to say that. I wish they would. They don't all have the vision yet. I'm praying that they will. I think some people joined Black Sheep HDFC because it's kind of convenient to ride with other Chris-tians and not do all the drinking and drug scene. Like maybe some of the motorcycle clubs do.

Barbara had much stronger feelings regarding the types of mission work and activities and the extent of participation from all members. She replied to these questions in this way:

> I don't think some people see it as a ministry. I think some people see it as more or less a social event. I'm not even sure that I under-stand the mission completely. I know we have focused on HOG members, but I know there's so much more we could be doing that we're not. There are so many different things that Christians could be putting their hands into and it's not necessarily that everybody in the Black Sheep have to participate. People don't necessarily relate to us as much and maybe we need to be out there open to them, so they can be open to us. As far as activities and such we support the local HOG chapters. But outside of blessing of the bikes, I don't really see that they've done anything.

Nathan maintains that not all people understand the mission of Black Sheep and vary in their involvement "because people are so varied. Our life experiences pretty much dictate how we feel and think about things. We all have vast differences in life experiences." While Nathan clearly understands the mission of Black Sheep HDFC he does not have a very clear idea of either the activities of Black Sheep or its mission work.

> I haven't been around in a while. I know we still do our breakfast meetings. We have rides to different areas where we have lunch. We do things for different people in the organization. We do community service. I think we're still having a biker church. Then we have our fellowship.

As far as mission work he answered with "currently I couldn't answer that. But I do know that the mission of Black Sheep is to bring Christianity to HOG members" In regard to whether all members participates in the Black Sheep activities Nathan maintains that involvement is:

> sporadic. It's not our way of life. Black Sheep as a motorcycle club or motorcycle ministry is different from your typical bikers where their way of life is their bike and organization.

Elizabeth is not concerned with the details of the mission of Black Sheep but with people's attitudes toward Christ.

> I would just say it is human nature that people have a different outlook on Christ, outlook on religion, outlook on people, bikes, places, and things. But if the whole group understands that the mission is Jesus Christ, then we agree.

Elizabeth is the secretary of a Southern California chapter of Black Sheep, yet she does not appear to have a good understanding of the mission and activities of the club. She describes the activities of Black Sheep HDFC as "well, they get together and they show the patch."

Kate knows the mission of Black Sheep and feels that the club is fairly successful in achieving its goal.

> The mission of Black Sheep HDFC is to serve and share the gospel with HOG members. I think we look like HOG members. I think that's the image that we portray. I think we are friendly and helpful and open and I think that's why the HOG members always approach us. But I think there is a lot of Black Sheep members that want to be part of Black Sheep but it's a fellowship group for them. They are not really in it, you know, to serve the HOG members. They don't want to volunteer at the barbecues or go on the HOG rides, you know, do things like that. They want to just fellowship at the Black Sheep breakfast and those kind of things. I don't think everybody really gets it.

Kate describes the activities and mission work of Black Sheep as:

Our chapter breakfast that we have is definitely an outreach because the majority of people that come are not Christians. Most of them are HOG members or people that come from other places. We put fliers up at all the local dealerships and we pass out fliers at biker events. Sometimes at our chapter breakfast, we have like sixty people show and then sometimes we only have eight people show. Besides the outreach, such as our chapter breakfast in which the gospel is presented in a non-threatening way, we also do HOG stuff. I think one of the cool things we do is to go on the HOG rides and to help out at the different HOG events because then we are developing relationships with people. It is kind of like a bridge building ministry. Where you build bridges with people through service to them, and then you're able to be part of their lives and to share Christ with them as a friend. Friendship evangelism is way more effective than soap box preaching.

In regard to whether all members are equally active in the Black Sheep ministry Bill claims that:

the Black Sheep is not any different than the church at large. I believe that the church claims that about 20 percent of the people in a church do all the work and they come for the right reasons and the other 80 percent are just hanging on and having fun. I'm certain that that happens as well in Black Sheep. But I don't have a problem with that. Because I'd rather carry the other 80 percent until they feel that pull on their heart to participate. So I'll do that as opposed to feel bitter about them.

Amy is rather forward and direct in both the way she answers questions and leads her life. She describes the mission of Black Sheep in the following way.

The mission statement of Black Sheep is a family oriented Christ centered motorcycle club specifically aimed at HOG members. But I don't think I have the passion for it that Marty has. Of course, give me opportunity I'll share Christ with anybody who wants to know. I still doubt myself. I still doubt my witness sometimes.

Amy does not think all members expect the same things from the Black Sheep and describes how her expectations have changed over time.

We're all different people. We don't see things the same. When I first started with Black Sheep, I think I saw the group differently than what I see them now. I'm now more interested in seeing other bikers come to know Christ than I was when I first started riding. I think they may all [members] know the mission. I think that we're all at different levels in our Christian walk, and in our understanding of the mission of Black Sheep. So we're all at different levels of capability of reaching that goal. Some of us are still in the "I need stage." We still need Black Sheep's help. Others of us are ready to give to Black Sheep and other bikers.

Consistent with the information derived from the questions on the positives and negatives of the group many of the members recognize the lack of participation from all members. However, it is rather noticeable that many members understand the mission of Black Sheep, but not how it is actually achieved. They were unable to describe the activities and mission work of the group. This highlights the statements some members made in regard to Black Sheep HDFC only being a social group for some members. Interestingly, two comments were made that perhaps bring to light reasons for some members seeing the Black Sheep HDFC as only a social club. The first is the longer a member is part of Black Sheep HDFC the more aware and more active in the mission work they become and the other is not all members see Black Sheep as a way of life—an identity. Clearly, many of the members do not see Black Sheep Harley-Davidsons for Christ mission work and activities as important elements in their identity as a Christian biker.

Black Sheep Image

The next area of questions pertained to the image both the Black Sheep HDFC Motorcycle Ministry as a group portrays and the individual respondent portrays. The purpose of asking these questions was to examine how the respondents viewed themselves as bikers, how they saw the role of Black Sheep Harley-Davidsons for Christ Motorcycle Ministry in the biker world and their personal role in the ministry. The first three questions examined the respondents' image and attitude of the Black Sheep HDFC club, the next three questions tackled information about feeling and looking like rough and tough bikers and how others view them and the Black Sheep HDFC club, the questions following those explored if any of the respondents felt embarrassed to be seen as bikers or as Christians. In regard to how other people see the Black Sheep HDFC Motorcycle Ministry Marty responds with this:

> Well, there's a big misunderstanding about what motorcyclists are all about. People who are not motorcyclists and especially church people look at Black Sheep and see a pretty hard, rough and tough group of guys and gals. But when we're seen in the context of HOG, we just fit in. When we're seen in the context of places like Laughlin and Sturgis and Hollister, which are major biker events in the course of a year, we're almost seen as soft. I hope that our image is neutral in the motorcycle world; we are not trying to call attention to anything about us, except that people would see the joy in our hearts, a level of integrity and purity in our way of living. We do have a few things on our patch that make a statement, a positive statement, whether it's a large patch across our shoulders that states "Jesus is Lord" or simply the element of our main patch that says 'I'm not ashamed of the Gospel.'

Marty resents when members of Black Sheep try to look rough and tough. He maintains that is just not what Black Sheep is all about.

> I mean, a Christian guy, who five days a week is a teacher or business person or a woman who is a housewife and on weekends they're going to become this leather clad, tough person. Yeah, some do that. I resent it. I think this is a fantasy for some people. They get to break out of the humdrum. Now all of a sudden you're doing this dangerous thing. And it's a bit of a rebellion against the norm. That's not all wrong and bad.

Marty has had some people tell him that they do not want to join Black Sheep because it is too bold of a Christian statement.

> Some of them have actually verbalized that they were embarrassed of being a fanatic or being a crazy Christian or something like that. There is some limited repercussion that comes from that. Sometimes I see people snickering. I have been minding my own business in a restaurant and notice someone staring or snickering. I've had people flip me off on the freeway. I've had people try to run me off on the freeway. Maybe it's my own paranoia. Just because they're after me doesn't mean I'm paranoid. It seems I can tell the difference between somebody who didn't see me and did a dumb thing and cut me off and the person who was trying to make a statement. The only two things they could be making a statement about is that I'm a motorcycle rider and they don't like motorcycle riders or that I'm a Christian. I have large, four inch, gold letters on my back that say "Jesus is Lord." I have really taken it personally sometimes when I thought people were making a statement about Christians.

The responses from the members differ a bit from Marty. Wayne explains his opinion in this way:

> Well, I think it's a mixed image because if you see them just riding down the road, you know, I'm sure that people have all different concepts of what the Black Sheep are and what they represent. I think it's as soon as they open their mouth, that's when the image is portrayed. I think when people see us their first thought is, "oh, not another biker gang." However, if they have any interaction with us they find out we're Christians and we're out there to basically promote Christ and to improve the community and the image of people who ride Harley-Davidson. I think we portray Christianity in a good light. I don't know how Black Sheep could do it any different. To be accepted in the biker world, if that's what you want to call it, you have to, in some ways, be a part of that culture.

Wayne maintains that sometimes people want to be seen as rough and tough and often are, whether they want to or not, because of the clothing and the bike it just happens.

I think at some point anybody that dons the biker attire and gets the bike wants to portray that image for their own personal reasons, whatever that might be. I think when you look at a biker all dressed up in their leathers, yeah, they can look pretty bad. Their appearance can really demonstrate that. But I think most cases, when they open their mouth, you see the genuine person, you know. And that bad image goes away. I think some members want to be seen as rough and tough but some members in Black Sheep obviously come from pretty tough backgrounds and maybe that's an image that possibly they're comfortable with.

While Wayne believes that some of the members come from "pretty tough" backgrounds, Barbara think the very opposite. She has more of a negative attitude toward the image Black Sheep HDFC Motorcycle Ministry portrays. She claims that Black Sheep are seen as more "pseudo bikers" than "real bikers." She notes that:

Very few of them are very hard core riders that really like to get on their bikes and ride them hard. That's where the other motorcycle clubs and gangs kind of make fun of us. I think that a lot of members join the Black Sheep for the patch. We all dress up in the black leathers. But anybody who is riding a motorcycle can dress up in black leather. I think sometimes the Black Sheep are not taken very seriously. I think we need to do some serious work to boost up our image because people kind of laugh at us. Gee, we are just like a bunch of Christians hopping on motorcycles and riding around wearing patches.

As far as looking rough and tough Barbara maintains that she already looks that way: "I already do. It's just my presence." She believes that part of the reason some people join the Black Sheep is to look tough. "It's all part of a motorcycle culture." David has no idea what image Black Sheep HDFC portrays but believes:

the image that they are supposed to portray are people who love God and like motorcycles, who don't drink to get drunk, who don't do drugs to get loaded, who care about other people, are compassionate towards other people, generally as Christians period. We try to ride as people of integrity. I think really for the most part we are.

David has questioned whether some of the members are embarrassed to be seen as Christian bikers and admits to sometimes being confused about this himself. He states:

I've wondered about whether people are embarrassed to be Christian bikers. I don't know their heart. But I wonder sometimes when I don't see their patch on when it should be. I've wondered if they're embarrassed. I hope not. Originally I wasn't really sure if I wanted to be an evangelist riding a motorcycle. When I first got the Harley, I had no intention of being an evangelist on a Harley. I wanted a Har-

ley for the fun and riding in the wind, riding with my wife. Then, I
had made up my mind that the most important thing right now in my
life is Christ. It's simple. It's easy and it's natural.

Nathan responds to the question about wanting to look tough and rough by say-
ing "I don't need to. I don't really care what people think about me. Most people
ride Harleys because of that rough and tough stuff. It gives them a tough image." Nathan believes that there are people who are opposed to having a Christian motorcycle group. He claims that:

> one of the reasons why we chose Black Sheep as our name is because
> we don't fit in with the main population of church goers or Christian-
> ity and that's because we are out there. Yet, we don't fit in with the
> bikers because we're Christians.

Elizabeth thinks non-members do not really understand what the Black Sheep
HDFC ministry is.

> I think some people just don't understand. They think Black Sheep is
> kind of strange—the oxymoron of the Christian biker. I've actually
> had people ask me if the Black Sheep go out there and beat people up
> and tell them they had better believe in God. This is because it
> doesn't fit the form, doesn't fit the mold of how Christians quote
> "should be."

Bill claims that people sometimes see him as scary.

> I've had to explain to people that I have a job and I do not have a
> criminal record and that I'm a law abiding person because they just
> met me and all they see is leather and shaved head and beard and
> something scary. I like people to know that it don't matter what we
> look like, biker, not biker, we're basically just human beings.

The only time Bill is embarrassed to be seen as a Christian is when other
Christians are acting in non-Christian ways. "The only time I'm embarrassed to
be a Christian is when another Christian does something foolish and reflects on
all of us. Then I'm embarrassed that I'm identified as a Christian but not embarrassed to be a Christian."

Doug believes the image that Black Sheep portrays is that of "weird bikers."
He claims that "Christ was seen as odd. And I think that followers of Christ will
probably also be seen as odd because we're not to be 'of this world.' So if the
world sees us as Christ was seen I think we're on the right path." In response to
the question do you think Black Sheep members can be stuck between their
Christian beliefs and their desire to have fun, Doug claims, "I don't think they're
mutually exclusive. I think being Christian is fun. Sin is for a season."

Roger claims "that he has been embarrassed to be seen as a Christian. I
think people are going to think I'm weird, a Bible thumper, or a freak."

In regard to the image that Black Sheep portrays Chris claims he is sometime embarrassed when members try to act "cool."

> I think there are a lot of wanna-be's in the group. I always worry about the image because I just see a lot of people that, you know, aren't representing what the club is truly about. For example, you see these guys all dressed in black and they think they're really cool and everything. When I see members of the group doing something stupid that kind of embarrasses me.

Amy laughs at the way the Peter Jennings spot described the Black Sheep.

> Well, Peter Jennings said we were hardcore bikers, which made me laugh when I look and think about some of our members. I think the image Black Sheep portray depends on who you are asking. Because my friends at work, they know I'm a biker. They just think I'm this crazy biker chick that goes to church.

Amy claims she already looks rough and tough. "I don't need a bike to make me look that way." Sometimes Amy gets stuck between her desire to have fun and her Christian beliefs. "Sometimes I've gone ahead and had my fun and felt guilty for it later. But I still felt like a Christian and I had fun."

Ernie is another member who contends that he looks: "rough and tough whether I'm in Black Sheep or not." Larry does not believe that other members of Black Sheep want to look rough and tough. "I think they want to have a sense of belonging to something. Everybody wants to belong to something."

John believes that the image the Black Sheep portrays is:

> a great image. They portray to people that they're Christian motorcyclists. I don't know that they portray a Christian biker. I think they want to, but they don't. I think they want to portray a biker, but they don't. They will befriend you and deliver the gospel in a real down-to-earth way that people can understand without, you know being taken aback by it. Before I was a Christian, I was approached by all kinds of different people that were wanting me to be a Christian. I didn't respond to any of them. The reason I didn't respond is because it was always connected with "you're a sinner, you're going to hell if you don't do this." Someone who is not a Christian doesn't understand they're a sinner. They don't believe they're a sinner. Everyone thinks they're a good person. They may not believe in hell and don't know the concept of hell. And that's that common thing that is projected out. "You have to believe or you're going to hell." That may be true, but that's not the way it should be delivered to people initially. I think Black Sheep does a great job delivering it to people on the level that is more compassionate-based, and love-based without the whole sinner/hell thing.

John thinks that many Black Sheep want to be seen as bikers.

I think they want to be seen as bikers. I think that's unfortunate, because I think most people in America, their idea of a biker is not the
Black Sheep or HOG or any of the other clubs. I think biker is often
associated with negativity. I don't think being considered a biker is a
positive thing. If somebody said to me, "oh, you're a biker," I
wouldn't be embarrassed by it, but I would correct them. I would
say: I'm not a biker; I love to ride motorcycles, but I'm not a biker.

Many members felt that Black Sheep HDFC members portray a good image. Most agree that overall at first glance they may appear to look rough and
tough but once people read the patch and spend time speaking with them any
negative image dissipates. It is obvious that some members may want to give off
the image of a rough and tough biker, but most of the respondents did not feel
any Black Sheep member could actually pull that image off for any length of
time. However, because some members come from either outlaw backgrounds
or rougher backgrounds they may be mistaken for the rough and tough biker.
Interestingly, most of the members seemingly blamed the other members for
being wannabe rough and tough bikers and when questioned about their own
appearance it was explained as being necessary for the sport of motorcycle riding. The next area of questions explores the perception other bikers, and Christians, have toward Black Sheep HDFC.

Perceptions of What Others Think

How others perceive the Black Sheep should have an effect on how each member and the overall group view themselves. Furthermore how others perceive the
Black Sheep should also have an effect on how the members play their role as a
Black Sheep member and when, how, and under what circumstances the role is
activated. The following covers the questions that pertain to image both internal
and external to the respondent. Some people are opposed to the Black Sheep
HDFC Motorcycle Ministry. Marty maintains because:

they don't understand the motorcycle culture. More often than not
they have put moral value to amoral issues. You know, why would
that person have long hair? Why would that person wear those dark
glasses? Why do they have earrings in? Why do they have tattoos?
I know a pastor friend of mine who's an overseer, superintendent or
whatever he is, and was vocal from the pulpit that pastors should not
be riding Harley-Davidsons because of the bad boy image that is associated with Harley-Davidsons. I mean, next thing you know, we
won't be able to ride in pickup trucks because of the bad connotation
of pickup trucks or something.

Wayne thinks other Christians may be opposed to the concept of Black
Sheep HDFC Motorcycle Ministry because "of the motorcycle culture and what
it has represented throughout history. There's always been that bad boy, the bad
guy image." Barbara believes that other Christians are not necessarily opposed

to Black Sheep HDFC but they probably "look at us differently than just your standard Christian." She continues with a story.

> My stepmother who professed to be a Christian was really the biggest bitch there ever was and back in the early '80s, Trinity Broadcast Network (TBN) started playing Christian music and music videos. Ernie and I thought this music was a wonderful thing and it opened us to all different types of Christian music. My stepmother thought that they had no business playing that kind of music so she stopped giving to TBN. So my point is that there is a lot of Christians out there like my stepmother who believes that unless you fit into the Christian box that the old establishment has created, that, you know, you're not on the right track. Although, I can't see why some Christians would be opposed to Black Sheep because the Bible says to go out and tell the world about Jesus. You have to approach people differently.

Kate hasn't personally found any criticism from non-Black Sheep members about the ministry except "somebody who told my daughter that she thought a Christian motorcycle club was wrong, because people who ride motorcycles are bad people and that we were, you know, imitating bad people."

Bill feels that some Christians may be opposed to the Black Sheep because "they are conservative Christians that are afraid of any radical change and any radical thoughts or any difference in what they consider to be Christian norm."

Amy does not think overall people have a problem with Black Sheep HDFC Motorcycle Ministry.

> I think sometimes at first people might not know what to think. I have been pretty amazed because even old farts, they like us. Sometimes some people just have to have something to look down their nose at and Black Sheep is a good one. You know. They can complain that we hang around with sinners.

Brad believes that non-Christians are bound to be uncomfortable with the Black Sheep HDFC because "of us being a group of Christians. In any Christian club or activities, occasionally people who are non-Christians would be uncomfortable in that atmosphere."

John explains that there is always some group of people that don't like another group of people especially in the Christian world.

> Christians are an interesting group because you could have one segment that sees guys trying to be bikers and calling themselves Christians as negative toward Christianity. Somehow there are sending the wrong sign and trying to be like the world. Then there are other groups of Christians that would say that's fantastic because you're not trying to be like the world; you're going into the world to deliver the message. It just depends how they see it.

Regardless of the image they portray or believe they portray it does not seem to be a problem for the members I interviewed. Most felt that it was out of their hands and hoped that their behavior would speak for itself.

How Did You Learn To Be a Biker

Similar to the questions in Chapter five regarding learning how to be a Christian and the ease or difficulty of playing the role these following questions examine the role of the biker. These questions examined how the respondents have learned the role of the biker, the ease or difficulty of the role, and how they define themselves as bikers. However, while the question regarding how the respondents have learned to be a Christian, in Chapter five, brought forth compliments as being a great question, the question regarding how the respondent learned how to be a biker had the opposite effect. I was told numerous times that it was a stupid question. Apparently, one can learn to be a Christian, but not a biker. I also received a few sarcastic remarks; for example: Marty claimed he learned how to be a biker when he bought a book called "10 Steps on How to Become a Biker."

Barbara did not believe people learn how to be bikers. She answered by asking a question.

> Do people actually learn that? I'm thinking I'm the same person before the motorcycle as I was after the person with the motorcycle. Other than I put on a pair of heavy-duty boots. The role or persona is not hard to portray. I imagine for some people it's like an act, but for me it's just natural. Heck, I am just the backseat driver.

David doesn't consider himself a biker in the sense of the stigma there is about bikers like you see on television.

> Gee whiz. I consider myself to be kind of a preppy biker, because I didn't come up through the biker ranks. I consider myself a good biker, if there is such a thing. I am still learning to ride. I am just a sixty-two year old white person riding a motorcycle.

Elizabeth sees herself as a seasoned biker and defines herself as a "seasoned biker." Kate answers the question about how she defines herself as a biker in this way:

> I think I'm a biker like I'm a Christian. Whereas they're so tied together that they're the same thing. When I became born again is also when I became like a lot of people define me as being punk rock. You know that's how they define me through the years as being punk rock, because I've had my hair in a Mohawk. That's who I am and because I'm not conformed to this world. I look different and I think different. I have a hard time with rules and things like that because I don't want to have to be tied down to things. I don't like being tied to

anything in this world. So, I fit as a biker. I fit as a punk, against the establishment, against the world, kind of thing, because that was born in me when I was born again.

Consistent with the others, Bill asserts that:

I've never changed. I've always been the same. The only wardrobe change that I underwent a year ago was shirts that carried the Harley logo. But before that I always just wore jeans, boots and T-shirts the only difference is that I ride a Harley. That I would define myself as a biker, I'm just a guy that rides a bike that likes to camp.

Roger maintains that he learned how to be a biker from:

emulating fellow bikers. In 1970 on my first Harley, I was influenced and inspired by a program called Then Came Bronson. Yeah, that really played a big part in me wanting a Harley-Davidson. He was a lone biker that used to travel across Wyoming and the movie *Easy Rider*, Peter Fonda, and Dennis Hopper. Also my high school friends at the time, a few of them started getting Harleys. And that motivated me to get one.

Chris learned how to be a biker from hanging out with other bikers. He claims that:

I didn't learn. I just started riding motorcycles. Motorcycle riders just kind of congregate together. Birds of a feather, you know. And next thing I knew I was—of course, those were my party days. I was in places where bikers were and congregating and partying with them. You know, it's just something that you do. I don't think you learn it.

Amy, like many of the others, defines herself as a biker in this way. "The same way I define myself as a Christian. A biker isn't who I am. A biker is something I do. A Christian is what I am—a child of God. For me it just fits." Brad, like many others, doesn't believe he ever learned how to be a biker. He states:

I don't know that I ever learned how to be a biker. I don't know that that's something that you do. I just enjoy riding motorcycles, although, in all honesty, I would not ride a motorcycle on the street probably if it wasn't a Harley-Davidson. If I didn't have a Harley-Davidson, I probably wouldn't ride.

Ernie claims:

anybody can dress up in leather and look like a tough guy if they want to. I'm not a hard core biker. I used to ride as a guest with the Hells Angels. I think I'm experienced enough and put enough miles

on it that I know how to handle my bike but I don't have a bad boy
biker attitude.

All fifteen respondents maintained that if they had to choose between being
a Christian and a biker they would choose Christian. Examples of the answers to
this question are: "fortunately my God does not require me to choose," "well, I
could stop riding a bike, but that would not change who I am," "absolutely a
Christian that's who I am," and "I'd still be a Christian whether I had the bike or
not, when called upon, I am who I am and that never changes." "It doesn't
make any difference. I am who I am and I do not adjust my Christianity for
anybody," and "well, Christian. Did you have anybody answer biker?"

Conclusion

This final data chapter brought to light some very interesting information especially when tied to the earlier data. How the members became part of Black
Sheep HDFC was typical. Many found out about the group through the church,
newspapers, fliers, and at biker events. The reasons why the respondents became
part of the Black Sheep were of particular interest. Many members maintained
they joined Black Sheep because they were looking for a place to belong and to
be with like thinkers. Others wanted to use their motorcycles as a way to witness
to non-believers about Jesus. Most importantly is that many of the respondents
claimed that they were outsiders most of their lives and wanted to be part of a
group. All of the respondents maintained that often they did not blend within the
boundaries of traditional Christianity and the Black Sheep HDFC was a good fit
for them. A lot of the members described themselves as "coloring outside the
lines."

The need to feel like part of a group is of great interest and a common
theme found throughout this research. Many of the members claim they have
never felt as if they belonged, they stated they had always felt like an outsider.
The Black Sheep is described by many of the members as a group where you are
accepted regardless of your background. In short, many of these members have
felt like outsiders in the secular world and within traditional Christianity and
they have found Black Sheep HDFC as a place to become an insider.

When the respondents were asked about the mission of Black Sheep HDFC
most were able to explain in detail that the mission was to bring Jesus to the
non-believers in the HOG organization. However, when asked what types of
mission work that the group actually performed for HOG, few were able to provide this information. Surprisingly, most members were only able to discuss the
Black Sheep activities such as national and chapter meetings and various rides,
but no actual mission work. This could be partly due to members not recogniz-
ing the true mission of the group. Granted they were able to articulate the mission but if they are not active in the mission work they must either not support
the mission work, not actually understand the mission work, or do not want to be
part of that aspect of the group.

All the members agreed that Black Sheep is a great group and is a great way to "spread the Gospel." Many maintain it was great to ride with clean and sober riders and with like-thinkers. However, in regard to the negative aspects of the group many complained that there were only a few members doing all the work. This gives credence to the complaints from some respondents about the lack of one hundred percent participation from the group in regard to the mission work. Others complained that some members think Black Sheep is a social club. Members viewing Black Sheep as a social club could explain why many of the respondents were unable to describe the mission work and could also explain the lack of participation in mission activities on the part of some members.

The image that the respondents felt the Black Sheep portrayed was good. Although, many recognized that the garments the members wear to stay safe on the bike could produce a rough and tough appearance. Most maintain that once people spent some time with them and read the patch any negative image would disappear. Other believed that some members want to look like rough and tough bikers but claimed that those members were wannabes. However, they personally never wanted to look rough and tough and if they did they claimed it was only due to the nature of the sport or due to how they look generally.

How the members learned to be bikers was apparently a stupid question and most were unwilling or unable to answer the question. Interestingly, they were able to discuss how they learned to be Christians but not bikers. As far as the ease or difficulty of playing the biker role, none of the respondents appeared to be concerned and felt riding a Harley-Davidson motorcycle is just a fun thing to do.

Another interesting theme that came out in this chapter is how the respondents identified, as Christians or biker. Again, it was as if I was asking a very stupid question. They all responded with Christian first and foremost. There was never any hesitation or doubt. While they play the role of the Christian biker and the role provides them with a place to belong it is not their most salient identity in their perspective. They may like the image of the biker but when push comes to shove they are Christians.

CHAPTER SEVEN

Conclusion and Discussion

Harley-Davidson motorcycles are now commonplace in mainstream America. One can expect to find at least one Harley-Davidson motorcycle in virtually every community in middle-class America. Owning a Harley symbolizes a freedom and rebellion that many owners want to experience outside the humdrum of their everyday life. This has been made possible by a shift in the image of the Harley rider from a deviant outlaw to a more romanticized rebel. Over the last twenty years Harley-Davidson has taken a failing company and turned it into a prospering business that has made the Harley-Davidson an icon of American life. The Harley-Davidson is as American as baseball, hot dogs, and apple pie.

Potential buyers of the Harley-Davidson motorcycle are encouraged through the enticing marketing and advertising techniques utilized by the Harley-Davidson Corporation to become part of a "family" of Harley owners. The company's advertising and marketing have managed to make the ownership of a Harley-Davidson motorcycle a high priority for many motorcycle enthusiasts who want to buy into this lifestyle. The Harley-Davidson Corporation maintains that for individuals to be part of this special "family," all that is necessary is to purchase a Harley-Davidson motorcycle and, of course, all the other paraphernalia associated with Harley-Davidson motorcycles. After these purchases are made one will then be a "biker."

What makes this so amazing is that twenty-eight percent of consumers purchasing a Harley today have never owned a motorcycle but are willing buy the motorcycle without even knowing if they enjoy the sport and with no experience as a rider.[1] This highlights how the creative marketing techniques of the Harley-Davidson Corporations have been able to shift the image of the sleazy, reckless, deviant outlaw biker of the 1960s into the romanticized biker of the twenty-first century. While this image shift has successfully toned down the deviant image of the Harley rider, there is still some confusion for many non-motorcycle enthusiasts (and motorcycle enthusiasts for that matter) as to who outlaw bikers are and who they are not. This is mostly due to the new group of riders co-opting the clothing, attitudes, and behaviors of the outlaw biker, thus creating a very similar appearance. Seemingly many of these new riders are looking to develop the cultural identity of the Harley rider making the ownership of the Harley-Davidson more about identity and image than about riding.

The more recent addition to the Harley "family," the Christian biker, specifically Black Sheep HDFC Motorcycle Ministry, embodies many of the same desires to be part of the Harley-Davidson motorcycle culture. Although most of the respondents in this study rode dirt bikes as children and young teens, many of the respondents have only recently become part of the Harley-Davidson motorcycle world with some actually buying Harleys just to be part of the Black Sheep HDFC Motorcycle Ministry. Many of the interview respondents identified as Christians, not bikers, yet most of the members interviewed refused to ride any motorcycle other than a Harley-Davidson. All of the Black Sheep members look like bikers, they wear the leathers, with many wearing both chaps and leather jackets, boots, t-shirts advertising Harley-Davidson products and any other garment that advertises Harley-Davidson. While many of the respondents have refused to define themselves as bikers they have seemingly co-opted at least the external persona of the biker. Furthermore, the name of the club Black Sheep Harley-Davidsons for Christ Motorcycle Ministry highlights the exclusiveness of the ministry to Harley riders. However, the group will argue that this Harley-Davidson exclusiveness is part of the focus of their ministry to serve the HOG members. In short, Black Sheep members must own and ride a Harley-Davidson motorcycle to be part of the ministry.

This research has focused on the how the identity of the Christian biker has been developed, maintained, and perpetuated through time. Beginning with Chapter Four this research has described how the Black Sheep HDFC Motorcycle Ministry began and its mission, general rules, and basic organization of the club. Understanding the fundamental framework of the ministry provided this research with a basic knowledge of what the ministry does and why it exists. Black Sheep HDFC Motorcycle Ministry consists of Christian people who ride Harley-Davidson motorcycles and follow an agreed upon set of rules, attitudes, and behaviors set forth by the ministry. This research found that Black Sheep HDFC focuses its ministry attention on HOG members in the community and provides them with a variety of different Christian services. The club is also known within the Harley "family" as a group that provides services such as free towing, church services, hospital visits, quilt ministry, and other types of activities including parade participation, local rides, and blood bank.

The interview schedule addressed the demographical, historical, and Christian trajectories of the Black Sheep HDFC interviewees and searched for patterns within and among the respondents. The members of Black Sheep are fairly close in age with forty-seven being the mean age of those interviewed. This supports the data reported by Harley-Davidson Corporation that states that the median age of the Harley-Davidson rider today is forty-six years of age. The Harley-Davidson Corporation maintains that the median income of the Harley owner is $80,000.[2] Two-thirds of the respondents surveyed from Black Sheep HDFC defined themselves as middle-class while the other third defined themselves as upper-middle-class, many of the respondents held typically high paying jobs such as architect, lawyer, ICU nurse, and general contractor which would suggest a higher income level than middle-class. Possible explanations for this difference could be lack of agreed upon definitions of what is middle-class and what is upper-middle class, or because the respondents were asked what they perceived to be their class position, not any concrete numerical representations which would have provided the researcher and the respondent with a more tangible framework to determine class status. Another explanation could be an unwillingness to divulge any type of income information. Regardless, the age and income demographics follow the information derived from other sources, specifically the Harley-Davidson Corporation.

Mission

Most respondents had a fairly clear understanding of Black Sheep's mission, but felt that the other members did not understand the mission. This mostly had to do with a lack of participation from all the members. However, while most of the members were able to articulate the mission, few were able to accurately or even superficially describe what types of missions and activities the Black Sheep supported. This was very surprising because the website, the membership contract, and every meeting thoroughly discusses the mission of Black Sheep HDFC Motorcycle Ministry.

Most respondents had positive feelings about the Black Sheep HDFC Motorcycle Ministry. Many felt that it was a good outreach for Christ, and a great way to use their motorcycle as a form of ministry. Many of the respondents enjoyed the opportunity to both evangelize and ride. Frequent comments by the respondents related to the unconditional acceptance of all members regardless of their background or what they have done. For many the unconditional acceptance was a main reason for joining the club.

The respondents' negative feelings toward Black Sheep HDFC had more to do with working within groups than anything fundamentally wrong with the group. Many complained that many of the members were not active enough and that only a few members did the work for the rest. Another complaint was that the members that did offer to help with various projects would rescind their offer to help at the last minute and give some excuse as to why they were no longer going to assist. This is an ongoing problem in any organization and certainly not unique to this group. Perhaps this lack of participation can be explained by exploring how the members understood the mission of Black Sheep. Since all members do not understand the mission of Black Sheep and have varying ideas as to what they expect from the group it may be unrealistic to expect one hundred percent participation on the part of the members.

If the members were not aware of the types of mission work and activities that Black Sheep engaged in how can it be expected that there would be one hundred percent participation on the part of the members? Many members did recognize that not all members had the right personalities to be evangelists yet still wanted full participation from all members. This could certainly create feelings of frustration on the part of the members that do most of the work.

Others noted that many members only joined Black Sheep for the social benefits. This is also tied to how the members understand the mission of Black Sheep HDFC and each member's particular personality. If one understands the group as only a social group then it stands to reason these particular members will not be active in the mission work. Furthermore if some members of the group are uncomfortable with evangelizing and doing certain types of mission work then they most likely will not participate in all mission activities.

Most members learned about Black Sheep HDFC through church, so most members were already practicing Christians when they joined Black Sheep HDFC. Others learned about Black Sheep HDFC through newspapers, fliers, swap meets, biker events and rallies. The reasons the respondents gave for joining Black Sheep HDFC were they wanted to ride with clean and sober riders, they wanted to evangelize utilizing their motorcycles, and they wanted to ride with like-minded riders. However, the most interesting theme found was that the respondents felt welcome and comfortable with other Black Sheep members and with the group as a whole. Many of the respondents discussed having either no friends, or having feelings of being different or alien; they had always felt like Black Sheep and wanted to feel like they were part of a group of people that were like them. These particular respondents found membership in Black Sheep HDFC to be a place to belong and not feel like an outcast.

Outsiders

Many of the respondents discussed having felt like outsiders throughout most of their lives and that Black Sheep HDFC, with its unconditional acceptance, has been a place for many of them to feel they belong. For example, childhood experiences brought forth interesting information in regard to divorce and other familial problems. Many of the members had been raised in homes in which divorce was commonplace, however, divorce was not all that commonplace in society, in general, at the time they were being raised in the 1960s. Since the 1960s the divorce rate has doubled from 2.1 per 1000 population to 4.1 divorces per 1000 population in 2000.[3] This high rate of divorce lends credibility to the concerns the respondents had about feeling different and alien as a child, a feeling that has continued through adulthood. Being a child of divorced parents in the 1960s was stigmatizing. At that time experts and commentators were predicting all types of potential problems for children from broken homes. Society was not prepared for the changes brought about by a rising divorce rate in the 1960s. Christian churches did not accept divorce, single divorced woman were seen as sexually promiscuous, and the children from these broken homes were seen as wild and out of control.

Several of the members felt their childhood home life was frustrating or dysfunctional at best. Many of the respondents had complaints of abuse, both physical/sexual and chemical in the family home. While this dissatisfaction with childhood may not be unique to the respondents, the pattern still exists. When tied to the divorce factor these elements could all play a role in how the respondents view themselves as outcasts.

The role of Christian biker was found to be an avenue for these members to feel part of a group and down play how often they feel "different" or an "outsider" in both general society and within traditional Christianity. Feelings of inadequacy are overcome for some through membership in Black Sheep HDFC Motorcycle Ministry because they can be both a Christian and co-opt the romanticized biker image promoted by the Harley-Davidson Corporation. Furthermore, the members of Black Sheep are able to hide behind the biker costume and take on a foreign persona of someone "different" yet "cool." They are outside the loop, yet they are inside the loop. This highlights the benefits of being a Christian biker because it gives the respondents who have felt like outsiders a way to accommodate their feelings of alienation and difference.

Image

In regard to image most the respondents thought Black Sheep HDFC had a good image. While many of the respondents maintained that some members may look rough and tough they claimed it was just the nature of the motorcycle culture. Most respondents felt that to be safe, a motorcycle enthusiast needed to wear a helmet, leathers, and gloves. Many of the respondents felt that when people read the patch and spoke to the individual members they soon realized that the group consists of Christians riding Harley-Davidsons. Many of the respondents discussed that they just looked like scary people and had always looked this way. Furthermore, many claimed they really have not changed their appearance to fit any type of biker image, but that they had always dressed and looked like bikers. In short, regardless of how they appear, most felt the patch and their actions portrayed a good image.

In regard to how others perceived the Black Sheep member and the club, there did not seem to be much concern from the respondents. Most felt that because the Black Sheep HDFC did not fit the "Christian mold" they were seen as alien or wrong. However, many of the respondents claimed that they never actually fit the "Christian mold," so membership did not really change how they were perceived by other Christians. This again brings forth the feeling of not belonging.

The interview schedule was used to question the respondents about how they learned to be a biker and how they defined themselves as a biker. The questions regarding how the respondents learned to be bikers seemingly was a very stupid question to most of the respondents and many told me so. Most respondents wanted to know if a person learns how to be a biker. Many claimed they never learned to be a biker, others claimed they just were around bikers and picked up their habits, and others actually admitted to learning how to be a biker on television and through movies (frankly I appreciated their honesty). Most respondents did not define themselves as bikers. They claimed that riding a Harley-Davidson was something they did, not who they were and being a Christian biker is just that—a Christian that rides a motorcycle.

Motorcycle experience overall appeared to be consistent from one member to the next. Most members rode dirt-bikes as young people and have bought Harleys as adults. Most respondents did not ride motorcycles of any kind for most of their adult life—the gap between teenage years and forty-something—while they were raising their children. What is interesting is that they have all decided to buy Harley-Davidsons now when only a couple had prior experience with this make and model of motorcycle. This leaves one to question the effects of Harley-Davidson marketing strategies, and the media and entertainment industry's influence on the purchasing/ownership of a Harley-Davidson. The few respondents that did not have prior motorcycle experience seemingly were unwilling to consider the ownership of any other make or model of motorcycle, again supporting the effects of marketing and the entertainment industry.

Most of the respondents have defined themselves as Christians for the better part of their adult life with most of them accepting Christ and the Christian belief system in their teenage years or as young adults. Only a couple of the respondents were actually new to Christianity. While most of the respondents accepted Christ at a fairly young age many of them claimed to have gone through times in their lives where Christ was not their main focus or when they left Christianity. Two claimed to have stayed steadfast in their Christian beliefs since the time they accepted Christ. The ways in which many of the respondents became Christians were unique with one accepting Christ under Montezuma's Revenge at Knott's Berry Farm Amusement Park, and another at a Jesus Freak concert in a park in Los Angeles. One woman accepted Christ after attending a Christian youth group only to be beaten when she got home and not allowed to attend church, and others accepted Christ at very young ages only to recommit at a later date.

Of particular interest is the high percentage of respondents (eighty-seven percent) that were raised with no practicing religion in the home. While some attended church and others were even educated in parochial schools, none of the respondents maintained that they had any form of the Christian religion practiced in the family home. Yet, today as adults, they are passionately Christian and involved with Christianity daily. They surround themselves with Christian people and stay involved with Christian activities.

With no religion practiced in the home the norms and values of Christianity needed to be learned in another manner. The respondents seemed to fall into three camps in regard to how they learned to be Christians. The first camp claimed that they learned how to be a Christian by watching other Christians and reading the Bible. The second camp maintained that one cannot learn to be a Christian but just are because once a person accepts Christ in their life He (Christ) will live the Christian life through them. The last camp claims they have not learned how to be Christians yet and felt that they were poor representatives of Christianity. All agreed that there are many people in the world that claim to be Christians but not all these people represent Christianity in a positive light. Often in the interviews the respondents discussed their frustration with people that claimed to be Christians, but behaved in ways that contradicted the Bible and the ways of Christianity. One member went so far as to say he does not let people know he is a Christian because of the negative connotations that come with that label.

Portraying the role of a Christian is related to how a person learns to be a Christian. One strain of thought argues that living the life of a Christian and portraying a Christian is not difficult because it is Christ, who lives within the Christian, who does the actual portraying, thus taking the responsibility off of the respondent and putting the responsibility, if you will, on Christ. The other strain of thought maintains that the role of Christian is very difficult and comes with a great deal of responsibility. This requires that the Christian must work to portray and put forth the right behavior that will be pleasing to Christ not necessarily in the mind of others. Learning the right behavior, to perform the role of Christian correctly, is accomplished through prayer, church activity, reading the Bible, and associating with other Christians. Because some of the respondents put their identity as Christians in the realm of spirituality these distinctions could be difficult or challenging when attempting to use identity theory to describe behavior.

The respondents all identified themselves as Christians and all wanted to perform the role of Christian well, whether the role is a result of their own doing or that of Christ. Most importantly, these respondents unanimously defined themselves as Christians and have thoughtfully developed a role to accommodate being Christian regardless of whether they believe Christ performs the role or they do. The respondents appear to be very committed to the Christian identity.

Two compelling themes emerged during these interviews. The first theme was that the respondents found Black Sheep HDFC to be a place to be accepted and a way to belong to a group. Many had felt like outsiders growing up and as adults and were looking for a place to feel like an insider as opposed to an outsider. Black Sheep HDFC has provided these respondents with a place in which to feel like an insider. In the secular world, the Black Sheep member is able to hide behind the biker costume and bike if they are rejected because they are a Christian. In the biker world, if the Black Sheep member is not accepted as a biker or are unable to play the role of biker sufficiently they are able to hide behind the role of Christian. They can play both the role of Christian and biker and because they are paradoxical, they can avoid those feelings of being either rejected or alienated because the identities are so different. If they do not feel accepted or comfortable in one role, they can rely on the other because they have the patch to portray their Christianity and the bike and the biker costume to portray them as rough and tough bikers. It is as if these dueling identities are a safety net to secure acceptance or at least some degree of respect in any give situation. While the identities of biker and Christian are distinct they appear to also be interchangeable; hence the dueling identities: the Christian biker.

Secondly, all the members defined, described, and wholly identified themselves as Christians first and foremost. Regardless of how the questions were asked the answers remained consistent. Regardless of age, time as a Christian, time in the biker community, gender, income, or anything else these respondents identified as Christians. They were verbally committed to the identity of Christian.

Identity Theory and the Christian Biker

Research supports the increasing awareness and desire for many in mainstream America to purchase a Harley-Davidson Motorcycle—much of this is a result of the marketing techniques of the Harley-Davidson Corporation. Harley-Davidson Corporation has specifically taken the stereotype of the rough and tough biker and has romanticized this image from a dirty sleazy stereotype into a free thrill-seeking person who wants to rebel against mainstream America.

Christian bikers, specifically Black Sheep Harley-Davidsons for Christ Motorcycle Ministry members have co-opted this romanticized image of the Harley rider and included an evangelist component. By incorporating the evangelist component to the Harley rider image Christian bikers have sought to develop and image that is rough, tough, rebellious and Godly. In relation to identity, the Black Sheep HDFC members have whole-heartedly taken on the external role of the Christian biker. They dress like traditional bikers, but fly a Christian patch with other patches such as "Jesus is Lord." This external role is connected to the social position and is a function of an individual's capacity to portray the role with any kind of effectiveness. This research has found that the more active a member is in the motorcycle culture as a Black Sheep member the more comfortable or effective they are in playing the role of biker. All of the respondents of this study have developed the identity of the Christian biker. The identity of Christian biker for these respondents is in direct relationship to their membership in the Black Sheep HDFC Motorcycle Ministry. The respondents have purchased the bike, the patch, and the clothing to support the external role of member of the Black Sheep HDFC Motorcycle Ministry. They have learned through the other members, not only the behavior associated with being a Christian biker, but the role of the biker, in general. They have also learned the role of the biker through other bikers, media, and the entertainment industry. The degree to which each respondent identifies as a Christian biker varies in relation to the interactional commitment (depth and breadth) and the affective commitment each respondent has developed with the ministry, its mission, and its other members.

However, identity which is usually internal is another important element in examining identity. Identity theory maintains that identity is tied to the meanings and expectations a person has with an identity. As Black Sheep members spend more time with the biker subculture the more internalized their identity becomes. Some members are more active in relation to the ministry work which exposes them to many members of the motorcycle culture. Therefore, the more active a member is within both the Black Sheep Harley-Davidsons for Christ Motorcycle Ministry and other groups including HOG the easier it is for them to perform the role both externally and internally.

Commitment to the role of Christian biker is a component of time spent with the identity and the emotional ties a person develops via relationships with other bikers and the culture overall. Again, the more time a Black Sheep member spends with other bikers the more committed they are to the group, therefore, the identity. However, if the Black Sheep member is not affectively committed to Black Sheep Harley-Davidsons for Christ Motorcycle Ministry the less likely they will have developed and affective commitment to the group. They can, however, feel affectively committed to the larger biker community based on time spent with bikers overall.

Whether a member of Black Sheep is highly committed to the Christian biker identity determines the salience of the identity. In the case of Black Sheep Harley-Davidsons for Christ Motorcycle Ministry, not all members were highly attached to the Christian biker identity or to the ministry overall. Commitment to the ministry was the defining component in regard to the Christian biker identity. Some members were committed to the overall biker identity, but not the Christian biker identity.

A final element of identity theory is self-knowledge. Serpe maintained that self—knowledge is "selective and creative."[4] In relation to Black Sheep respondents they all seemed to appreciate themselves as bikers—with most of them believing that they portray the biker well and felt confident in their identity as a biker. Overall, the identity of biker appears to be very salient regardless of interactional or affective commitment. Seemingly, most of the respondents were proud of their biker persona and willing to work to perfect the role.

Of greatest interest is the relationship between being a biker and a Christian. All of the members defined themselves as Christians first and foremost and maintained that being a Christian is who they are and not a reflection of interactional and affective commitment to an identity. They maintain that they became Christian immediately when they accepted Jesus Christ as their Lord and Savior (born again). Due to this immediate acceptance of an identity the trajectory to role identity and commitment is fast tracked.

The identity of biker was not a determinant of the identity of Christian. The respondents identified as Christians, not bikers. Some were willing to identify as Christian bikers, but not as only bikers. This distinction is important because of the incredible commitment to the Christian identity. Regardless of how the questions about Christian and biker identities were framed the respondents did not hesitate; they defined themselves as Christians. For these respondents, the Christian was the more salient identity. The commitment to the Christian identity was not a reflection of time spent as a Christian, or time spent with other Christians but as a point and time in the respondent's life in which the respondent became a Christian. This does not support the traditional concepts of identity, commitment, and salience. Theories addressing how individuals develop, maintain and perpetuate any given identity are seemingly not supported in the case of the Christian. Further research is needed to extract the role of Christian beliefs in the commitment to the Christian identity.

Commitment to membership in the Black Sheep HDFC Motorcycle Ministry is related to the respondents desire to be identified as part of the club, not the respondent's commitment to the Christian biker identity. Commitment to the Black Sheep member identity is a reflection of the respondents desire to be part of a group that consists of like-thinkers, clean and sober riders, and the appreciation of being accepted and belonging to a group. The commitment to the identity of Black Sheep member increases with time spent with the other members, feelings of acceptance in regard to both who they are and how they perform the role of biker. The identity of Black Sheep member, therefore, is merely a reflection of group membership. However, the probability of becoming more committed to the Christian biker identity and the mission work of Black Sheep HDFC Motorcycle Ministry is closely tied to increased commitment to the identity of Black Sheep member. These respondents have found a way to have the "safety net" of being a Christian and all that is defined through that identity and the excitement of being viewed as a "wild untamed biker." It could be argued that for some this is seen as the best of both worlds, Christian and secular.

Notes

1. http://investor.Harley-Davidson.com/demographics.cfm?locale=en_US&bmLocale=en_US.

2. http://investor.Harley-Davidson.com/demographics.cfm?locale=en_US&bmLocale=en_US

3. http://search.msn.com/results.aspx?srch=105&FORM=AS5&q=U.S.+Bureau+of+the+Census%2c+2000.

4. Serpe, 1991.

Selected Bibliography

Anderson-Facile, Doreen. 1994. "Women Who Ride Harleys." *Proceedings National Conference of Undergraduate Research.* Asheville, North Carolina: University of North Carolina.

Babbie, Earl. 1992. *The Practice of Social Research, Sixth Edition.* Belmont, California: Wadsworth Publishing Company.

Becker, Howard. 1963. *Outsiders: Studies in Sociology of Deviance.* New York, New York: Free Press.

Becker, Howard, Blanche Geer, Everett C. Hughes, and Anselm L. Strauss. 1961. *Boys in White: Student Culture in Medical School.* Chicago, Illinois: University of Chicago Press.

Black Sheep Harley-Davidson for Christ Motorcycle Ministry Website http://www.blacksheephfdc.org .

Blumer, Herbert. 1969. *Symbolic Interactionism.* Englewood Cliff, New Jersey: Prentice-Hall.

Burke, Peter J. 1980. "The Self: Measurement Implications from a Symbolic Interactionist Perspective." *Social Psychology Quarterly* 43: 18-29.

Campbell, Anne. 1984. *The Girls in the Gang.* Cambridge, MA: Basil Blackwell, Inc.

_____. 1990. "Female Participation in Gangs." *Gangs in America,* ed. C. Ronald Hoff. Newbury Park, California: Sage Publication, LTD.

Cast, Alicia D. and Peter J. Burke. 2002. "A Theory of Self Esteem." *Social Forces* 55: 881-897.

Christian Motorcycle Association Website. www.christianlink.com/clubs/cma/ .

Cohen, Albert K. 1955. *Delinquent Boys: The Culture of the Gang.* New York: Free Press.

Collins, Randall. 1988. *Theoretical Sociology.* Orlando, Florida: Harcourt Brace Jovanovich.

Cooley, Charles Horton. 1902. *Human Nature and the Social Order.* New York, New York: Scribner Publishing.

Daly, Kathleen and Chesney-Lind, Meda. 1988. "Feminism and Criminology." *Justice Quarterly* 5(4): 497-538.

Edwards, Marty 2000. *Black Sheep H.D.F.C. Pamphlet. Murietta, California: Black Sheep H.D.F.C..*

Feagin, Joe R., Anthony M. Orum, and Gideon Sjoberg, editors. 1991. "The Nature of the Case Study." *A Case for the Case Study.* Chapel Hill, North Carolina: The University of North Carolina Press.

Free Methodist Church http://www.freemethodistchurch.org/Magazine/Articles/Mar-Apr_2005/M-A_2005_BlackSheep.htm .

Gans, Herbert. 1962. *The Urban Villagers.* New York, New York: Free Press.

Goffman, Erving. 1961. *Asylums*. New York, New York: Doubleday Press.

Harley-Davidson Corporation (2006)

    1http://investor.harley-davidson.com/InvestorNews.cfm?bmLocale=en_US# .

    2http://www.harley-davidson.com/wcm/Content/Pages/home.jsp?locale=en_US .

    3http://investor.harley-davidson.com/demographics.cfm?locale=en_US&bmLocale=en_US .

    4http://www.harley-davidson.com/PR/MOT/2006/06_template.asp?locale=en_US&bmLocale=en_US .

    5http://investor.harley-davidson.com/StatementsBalanceSheets.cfm?locale=en_US&bmLocale=en_US .

Harley Owners Groups (HOG). 2006. http://www.hogchapters.com/trippin.html .

Hopper, Columbus B. and Johnny Moore. 1990. "Women in Outlaw Motorcycle Gangs." *Journal of Contemporary Ethnography* 18(4): 363-387.

_____. 1983. "Hell on Wheels: The Outlaw Motorcycle Gangs." *Journal of American Culture*: 58-64.

Jackson, Chris and Glenn D. Wilson. 1993. "Mad, Bad or Sad? The Personality of Bikers." *Personality and Individual Differences* 14(1): 241-242.

Klemencic, Dan., 1993. "Quality, Not Quantity, Determines How Many Motorcycles We Make." *The Enthusiast*.

Lemert, Edwin. 1951. *Social Pathology*. New York, New York: McGraw Hill.

Lofland, John and Lyn H. Lofland. 1995. *Analyzing Social Settings: A Guide to Qualitative Observation and Analysis*. Belmont, California: Wadsworth Press.

Lyng, Stephen and Mitchell L. Bracey Jr. 1995. "Squaring the One Percent: Biker Style and the Selling of Cultural Resistance." *Cultural Criminology*, ed. Jeff Ferrell and Clinton R. Sanders. Boston, MA.: Northeastern University Studies.

Macionis, John J. 2001. *Sociology, 8th Edition*. Upper Saddle River, New Jersey: Prentice Hall.

McCall, George J. and J.T. Simmons 1978. *Identities and Interactions*. New York, New York: Free Press.

Mead, George Herbert. 1934a. *Mind, Self and Society*. Chicago, Illinois: University of Chicago Press.

_____. 1938b. *The Philosophy of the Act*. Chicago, Illinois: University of Chicago Press.

Mercer, Jane R. 1973. *Labeling the Mentally Retarded*. Berkeley, California: University of California Press.

Messerschmidt, James W. 1995. "From Patriarchy to Gender: Feminist Theory, Criminology, and the Challenge of Diversity." *International Feminist Perspectives in Criminology*, ed. Nicole Hahn Rafter and Frances Heidensohn. Buckingham, MK: Open University Press.

Michner, H.A., and J.D. DeLamater. 1999. *Social Psychology, Fourth Edition*. Orlando, Florida: Harcourt Press.

Miller, Walter B. 1958. "Lower-Class Culture as a Generating Milieu of Gang Delinquency." *Journal of Social Issues* 14: 5-19.

Outhwaite, William and Tom Bottomore, eds. 1994. *Twentieth Century Social Thought*. Oxford, England: Blackwell Publishers.

Quinn, James F. 1987. "Sex Roles and Hedonism Among Members of 'Outlaw'Motorcycle Clubs." *Deviant Behavior* 8: 47-63.

Rafter, Nicole Hahn and Frances Heidensohn. 1995. "Introduction: The Development of Feminist Perspectives on Crime." *International Feminist Perspectives in Criminology*, ed. Nicole Hahn Rafter and Frances Heidensohn. Buckingham, MK: Open University Press.

Riley, Anna and Peter J. Burke. 1995. "Identities and Self-Verification in the Small Group." *Social Psychology Quarterly* 58: 61-73.

Saladini, A. and P. Szymezak. 1997. *Harley-Davidson History Meetings New Models Custom Bikes*. New York, New York: Barnes and Noble Books.

Serpe, Richard T. 1987. "Stability and Change in Self: A Structural Symbolic Interactionist Explanation." *Social Psychology Quarterly* 50: 44-55.

_____. 1991. "The Cerebral Self: Thinking and Planning about Identity-Relevant Activities." *Self-Society Dynamic: Cognition, Emotion, and Action*, eds. Judith A. Howard and Peter L. Callero. Cambridge University Press:New York, New York.

Serpe, Richard T. and Sheldon Stryker 1987. "The Construction of Self and the Reconstruction of Social Relationships." *Advances in Group Processes* 4: 41-66. Greenwich, Connecticut: JAI Press.

Scheff, Thomas. I. 1966. *Being Mentally Ill: A Sociological Theory*. Chicago, Illinois: Aldine Press.

Sheldon, Randall G., Sharon K. Tracy, and William B. Brown. 1996. "Girls and Gangs: A Review of Recent Research." *Juvenile & Family Court Journal* 21: 21-39.

Stets, Jan E. and Peter J. Burke. 2000a. "Identity Theory and Social Identity Theory." *Social Psychology Quarterly* 63: 224-237.

_____. 2002b. "A Sociological Approach to Self and Identity." *Handbook of Self and Identity*, eds. Mark Leary and June Tangney. Guilford Press.

Stryker, Sheldon. 1968. "Identity Salience and Role Performance." *Journal of Marriage and the Family* 4: 558-564.

_____. 1980. *Symbolic Interactionism: A Social Structural Version*. Menlo Park, California: Benjamin Cummings.

_____. 1987. "Identity Theory: Developments and Extensions." Pp. 89-104 in *Self and Identity: Psychological Perspectives*. London, England: Wiley. .

_____. 2000. Identity *Competition: Key to Differential Social Involvement. in Identity, Self and Social Movements*. Minneapolis, Minnesota: University of Minnesota Press.

Stryker, Sheldon and Peter J. Burke. 2000. "The Past, Present, and Future of an Identity Theory." *Social Psychology Quarterly* 63 (4): 284-297.

Stryker, Sheldon and Richard T. Serpe. 1994. "Identity Salience and Psychological Centrality: Equuivalent, Overlapping, or Complementary Concepts?" *Social Psychology Quarterly* 57(1): 16-35.

Thomas William I. and Dorothy Swaine Thomas. 1928. *The Child in America*. New York, New York: Knop.

Thompson, William E., and Joseph V. Hickey. *2002. Society in Focus, Fourth Edition*. Boston, MA: Allyn and Bacon.

U.S. Bureau of the Census. 2000. www.u.s.census.com .

Wallace, Ruth A. and Alison Wolf 1999. *Contemporary Sociological Theory: Expanding the Classical Tradition, Fifth Edition*. Upper Saddle River, New Jersey: Prentice Hall.

Waldrop, Judith., 1991. "Bikers Ride Into Middle Age." *American Demographics*, December: 15-16.

Watson, J. Mark., 1982. "Righteousness on Two Wheels: Bikers as a Secular Sect." *Sociological Spectrum* 2: 333-349.

Williams III, Frank P. and Marilyn D. McShane. 1994. *Criminological Theory*. Englewood Cliffs, New Jersey: Prentice Hall.

Index

About the Author

Doreen Anderson-Facile is an Assistant Professor of Sociology at California State University Bakersfield. She received her Ph.D. from University of California Riverside in 2003. Her teaching and research areas focus around crime and deviance.